I0644688

In *How Do I Launch Writing in the Elementary Classroom?* Ann Marie Corgill invites us as writing teachers to step inside her classroom to learn from the powerful and strategic moves she makes with elementary writers. She carefully guides us in how to lift, honor, and showcase our students' voices and ideas by creating a guidebook of purposeful moves to make in the classroom during the first few weeks of school. With organic classroom procedures, student-created charts and habits, and professional resources throughout, Ann Marie reminds us that our students' voices are valuable teachers in the room. This book will ignite, or reignite, your love for growing writers. You will leave wanting to try something new in your classroom the very next day!

—***Victoria Dotson***, *fifth-grade teacher, Chicago Public Schools; NCTE Elementary Teacher Cohort member*

Imagine there's a teacher just down the hall, a person of generous heart whose door is always open, someone happy to share the particulars of what makes her classroom hum. That's the gift Ann Marie Corgill offers in her marvelous book *How Do I Launch Writing in the Elementary Classroom?* I've known Ann Marie for thirty years, and her classroom does hum. I've never known a finer teacher, period. Her understanding of kids, writing, and teaching resides in the marrow of her bones. Ann Marie's book is enormously practical and, at the same time, continually reminds us what truly matters when working with young writers. This is an essential book for anyone who teaches writing.

—***Ralph Fletcher***, *author of* Tapping the Writer within: Practical Ways to Help All Students Claim Their Wri-dentity *(2026)*

Ann Marie invites us to think deeply and intentionally about how we cultivate and nurture the conditions for young writers to grow and evolve. Grounded in an unwavering belief in children as agentive creators, every page is a testament to that stance. Through images, words, and the authentic voices of children, she shows how a powerful community of writers is built with learners. From designing classroom spaces to honoring writers' identities, she calls us to center children in every decision. This is a timeless book—one I will return to each year as a way of staying grounded in a pedagogy that positions children as agentive learners.

—***Stella Villalba***, *educator and author of* Tell Me More: Conferring with Artists, Writers, and Storytellers *(2026)*

Be like Ann Marie Corgill by relishing her great new book! This State Teacher of the Year has mastered the art of teaching writing. This invitation to "enter" her classroom and observe her proven techniques is a treasure. It is a must-read for both new and experienced teachers.

—***Cathy Randall***, *Director Emerita, Computer Based Honors Program, University of Alabama*

How refreshing to read a book focused on the critical beliefs for supporting writers: identity, community, and engagement. In *How Do I Launch Writing in the Elementary Classroom?* Ann Marie Corgill shows us the specific actions she employs each day in her classroom that support these beliefs. The specific classroom examples allow you the privilege of spending time in Ann Marie's classroom alongside students right from the start, so you can see what happens when children and their thinking is recognized, valued, and nurtured. As Ann Marie writes, "I first ask the children what they need from me. I care about how they think and what they say. Their voices and ideas matter to me, above all else." All children deserve to have their voices to be heard and valued. Fortunately Ann Marie shows us how.

—***Matt Glover***, *consultant and coauthor of* How to Become a Better Writing Teacher *(2024)*

How Do I Launch Writing in the Elementary Classroom? is a question and an answer. Ann Marie Corgill opens with a metaphor—her elders tending to trees and plants—being fascinated by the root and branch patterns—like those of her students. She then makes reference to Paulo Freire: "What the educator does in teaching is to make it possible for the students to become themselves." Ann Marie invites the reader to the area rug, "the center of gravity" in her classroom, where teacher and students "gather to learn, talk, share, laugh, and wrestle with ideas . . . where community comes to life, and from it learners launch (multiple times a day) into meaningful reading and writing work." Other than her enviable learning spaces, what is most notable is that she honors each student's voice, home language, and the translanguaging of her multilingual students—all via teacher-writer authenticity. This book is a delightful story and guide.

—***Alfredo Celedón Luján***, *former NCTE President*

This resource offers more than an invitation—it's a call to intentional teaching that centers children in every decision. Grounded in an invitational approach, *How Do I Launch Writing in the Elementary Classroom?* highlights Ann Marie's essential ingredients of meaningful learning: care, love, joy, and trust.

Woven with practical wisdom and concrete examples, Ann Marie shows how relationships and instruction work hand in hand, guiding educators to believe that how we teach matters—and that every decision helps children grow, flourish, and become.

—***JoEllen McCarthy***, *literacy advocate and author of* Layers of Learning: Using Read-Alouds to Connect Literacy and Caring Conversations *(2023)*

In *How Do I Launch Writing in the Elementary Classroom?* Ann Marie offers step-by-step guidance for developing learning experiences that empower young people. With attention and care, she details how to build a community of writers centered around students' needs, desires and identities. Her practical know-how invites readers to "see" how this type of classroom supports all learning styles and teaches not just writing but also agency. In framing writing as purposeful, layered and multidimensional, students compose and create in a variety of formats. Throughout this book, Ann Marie guides teachers in mentoring writers through texts, minilessons, conferring moments, and writing routines. This book empowers educators to trust the writers in their care and to create conditions so that every child flourishes.

—***Kristin Ziemke***, *international educator and author of* Text and Tech: Reading All Ways in K–8 *(2025)*

Whether you're guiding students to write labels for the classroom library, create informational pieces, or take on classroom responsibilities, *How Do I Launch Writing in the Elementary Classroom?* offers concrete and creative examples for authentic writing across all subjects. This resource nurtures curiosity, confidence, and skill, inviting children to see themselves as writers who value their own voices and those of others, well beyond the classroom.

Roberta Price Gardner, *associate professor, Kennesaw State University; coeditor of* Reading & Teaching with Diverse Nonfiction Children's Literature: Representations and Possibilities *(2021)*

HOW DO I...

Launch Writing in the Elementary Classroom?

HOW DO I...

Launch Writing in the Elementary Classroom?

Ann Marie Corgill

NCTE
National Council of Teachers of English®
ncte.org

HOW DO I... BOOK SERIES

Staff Editor: Jon Reigelman
Developmental Editor: Franki Sibberson
Copy Editor: Michael Ryan
Cover Design: Jon Reigelman
Interior Design: Jon Reigelman
Photography: Ann Marie Corgill, Marvin Young

ISBN (print): 978-0-8141-0310-4
ISBN (epub): 978-0-8141-0311-1
ISBN (PDF): 978-0-8141-0312-8

It is the policy of NCTE in its journals, blogs, and other publications and platforms to provide a forum for the open discussion of ideas concerning the content and the teaching of English and the language arts. The views, opinions, and perspectives expressed in these publications and platforms are those of the author(s) alone and do not necessarily reflect the official policy, position, or views of NCTE, its staff, members, leadership, or board of directors.

NCTE provides equal employment opportunity to all staff members and applicants for employment without regard to race, color, religion, sex, national origin, age, physical, mental or perceived handicap/disability, sexual orientation including gender identity or expression, ancestry, genetic information, marital status, military status, unfavorable discharge from military service, pregnancy, citizenship status, personal appearance, matriculation or political affiliation, or any other protected status under applicable federal, state, and local laws.

Every effort has been made to provide current URLs and email addresses, but, because of the rapidly changing nature of the web, some sites and addresses may no longer be accessible.

Library of Congress Control Number: 2026945940

Throughout my teaching career, I've learned from a community of incredible educators who've both grounded and inspired the work I do. They've shaped my beliefs about the teaching of writing and have helped me become the teacher and learner I am today. The following quotes remind me to honor and celebrate the voices, the abilities, the lives, and the writing of the students in my care.

—Ann Marie

"For apart from inquiry, apart from the praxis, individuals cannot be truly human. Knowledge emerges only through invention and re-invention, through the restless, impatient, continuing, hopeful inquiry human beings pursue in the world, with the world, and with each other."

—Paulo Freire, *Pedagogy of the Oppressed* (1993 reissue), p. 72

"To teach in a manner that respects and cares for the souls of our students is essential if we are to provide the necessary conditions where learning can most deeply and intimately begin."

—bell hooks, *Teaching to Transgress: Education as the Practice of Freedom* (1994), p. 13

"Children show us where they are in the way they use the page, the information and the process, they show us in their choices of topics, statements about writing, and the ways in which they respond to the writing of other children or evaluate their own writing."

—Donald Graves, *Writing: Teachers & Children at Work* (1983), p. 286

"Cute ideas alone aren't good enough. The work we do is too important. Authenticity is the filter. . . . I'm interested in ways of teaching that have authentic, real world, life-long implications. I'm interested in ways of using literature that make a lasting impression."

—Shelley Harwayne, Lasting Impressions *(1992), p. 3*

"If nothing else, children should leave school with a sense that if they act, and act strategically, they can accomplish their goals-a sense of agency."

—Peter Johnston, *Choice Words: How Our Language Affects Children's Learning, Second Edition* (2024), pp. 2–3

"The four walls of your classroom can be the world we want, hope for, dream of, rather than the world we have now. It can allow children to practice the skills they need to create and to sustain a place where people are neither shunned nor labeled; a shared, public place in which every community member is treated as a free person, an invaluable person, a gifted and good and loved person."

—**Carla Shalaby**, *Troublemakers: Lessons in Freedom from Young Children at School* (2017), p. 180

"The belief that everyone has the capacity to write suggests that to grow writers, we must start with the writer. As teachers of young writers, we need to recognize that our 'writers start in different places' (*Professional Knowledge for the Teaching of Writing*, 2016) and sometimes in different languages. Each of our young writers comes to our learning environment with their own history and relationship to writing."

—**Tracey T. Flores and María E. Fránquiz**, *Cultivating Young Multilingual Writers: Nurturing Voices and Stories in and beyond the Classroom Walls* (2023), p. 4

"The essential elements of such teaching (culturally relevant teaching) involve developing conceptions of self and others that are based on accurate historical and social information; encouraging social relations that are communal, interdependent, equitable, and just; and developing conceptions of knowledge as socially constructed and open to intellectual challenge."

—**Gloria Ladson Billings**, *Culturally Relevant Pedagogy: Asking a Different Question* (1983), pp. 72–73

"My vision for the writing workshop is that it be a place where we all pool all that we know to help each other write well...We have writers on the bookshelves and writers at the desks next to us, and we are all learning how to learn from each other."

—***Katie Wood Ray***, Wondrous Words: Writers and Writing in the Elementary Classroom *(1999), p. 268*

"My job as a teacher is not to teach the curriculum or even just teach the students; it is to seek to understand my kids as completely as possible so that I can purposefully bend the curriculum to meet them."

—**Cornelius Minor**, *We Got This: Equity, Access, and the Quest to Be Who Our Students Need Us to Be* (2018), p. 101

"Seek to understand what the writer is trying to do. This may require you to do a great deal of listening. When working with young writers, your listening may in fact help them name the intention that will drive their writing. What you teach in the conference will evolve from a deep understanding of the writer's intent."

—Ralph Fletcher and JoAnn Portalupi,
Craft Lessons: Teaching Writing K–8, Second Edition *(2007), p.10*

"We need to reenvision and relook at what we define as basic. . . . In order for reading and writing to make sense to their lives and enrich their lives, children will need a whole lot more than 'basic skills.' We need to be looking for a higher literacy. Without such a literacy of thoughtfulness, basic skills have no meaning."

—Regie Routman,
Literacy at the Crossroads: Crucial Talk About Reading, Writing, and Other Teaching Dilemmas (1996), pp. 88–90

"We live in a period where there's no time for 'urgent-free pedagogy.' Our instructional pursuits must be honest, bold, raw, unapologetic, and responsive to the social times."

—**Gholdy Muhammad**, *Cultivating Genius: An Equity Framework for Culturally and Historically Responsive Literacy* (2020), p. 54

"Our lives as educators are full of rich and diverse experiences, but we cannot possibly have an understanding of every hand that has been dealt to our students. And if a comment arises in the class that offends our personal belief system and we fall into the trap of responding ourselves rather than allowing students' truths to be expressed, we are controlling the ownership of the learning. . . . Your strongest superpower in the classroom is kid watching. Make it about what the kids are doing and saying. That is, listen; don't just wait to talk."

—**Sara K. Ahmed**, *Being the Change: Lessons and Strategies to Teach Social Comprehension* (2018), p. xxvii

"If we are truly to build on children's natural creative abilities, we need to create a workshop of the possible in our schools-a workshop where it is possible for children to explore their obsessions, take risks in their thinking, and apprentice themselves to many other learners; a workshop where there is a shift in the locus of control in the classroom, from teacher to student, where students take more responsibility for the problems they choose to solve; a workshop where it is possible for children to create personal inventories of their knowledge and their stories, where they aren't expected to check their cultures at the door; a workshop where there is time for students to be the learners that they were born to be, and where we as teachers appreciate and delight in the extraordinary creative abilities of each child."

—**Ruth Shagoury**, *A Workshop of the Possible: Nurturing Children's Creative Development* (1996), p. 151

"Be who you are, breathe fully, be alive, and don't forget to write."

—**Natalie Goldberg**, *Wild Mind: Living the Writer's Life* (1990), p. 14

"Children need us as teachers on so many levels. Sure, we can be rigorous, but that doesn't mean rigorous in our service to external test scores.

It means rigorous in our service to children, and using our expertise to know where each of them is as a reader, a writer, and a thinker and where to take them next."

—**Sharon Taberski**, *Comprehension from the Ground Up: Simplified, Sensible Instruction for the K–3 Reading Workshop* (2010), p. 13

"What's love got to do with it? Everything. Everything. It's a term we do not like to talk about. It's not 'science-y' like pedagogy. The curriculum. The lesson plans. The amazing diverse literature that you put in someone's hands, means nothing if you do not love them."

—***Ernest Morrell***, *Presidential address at the 2014 NCTE Annual Convention*

Contents

Room for Writers to Grow

My mother and grandmother both shared a love of flowering trees and plants. They could somehow tend, nurture, and keep even the daintiest bloom or leaf alive and flourishing. They certainly knew a thing or two about caring for all things growing, right down to the roots. Although I don't have their green thumbs, I am fascinated by the root systems of trees . . . how they grow, their expansion patterns, and the factors that inhibit or enhance that growth. I'm equally fascinated by how children in our classroom grow and thrive.

Trees flourish in unrestricted spaces where their roots can easily find oxygen and nutrients. My teaching pedagogy in many ways mirrors the root systems of trees. I believe that the writers I teach and learn alongside grow and flourish in those unrestricted spaces, ones that fill their souls with oxygen and nourishment.

Over the lifetime of my teaching, Paulo Freire's work has grounded me. In *We Make the Road by Walking: Conversations on Education and Social Change* (1990) he says, "What the educator does in teaching is to make it possible for the students to become themselves." It's this idea that is central to every part of this book . . . that children deserve room to grow, to become themselves, in a space that honors their lived experiences, their languages, their literacies, their expertise, and all they bring to the classroom.

My pedagogical family tree runs deep and wide, and the routines, strategies, and beliefs I will share throughout this piece are grounded in and enhanced by the work of educators from across the country and globe (and even right next door!) for the past 30 years. I've kept this text short, but it's important for you to know that the practices I share do not stand alone and are shaped by many experts in the field. You'll find quotes from people who have ignited my learning and anchored my teaching since the day I stepped into the classroom. At the end of every section, you'll find professional texts to explore that will give you opportunities to deepen your understanding. These teachers and authors can provide the depth for you to linger and learn even more about the ideas I've touched on and the foundations on which I stand: Joy. Engagement. Trust. Sense-making. Authenticity. Choice. Autonomy. Agency. Intentionality. Honesty. Reflection. Communication. Connection. Culturally and linguistically sustaining practices. Whole child, asset-based instruction.

Thank you for coming along with me as I share our collective growth (the writers' growth and mine) over the first nine weeks of school. It's a beginning-of-writing journey where I'll share ideas, strategies, routines, and suggestions for how to launch writing experiences with a group of young learners while listening closely and honoring their voices through every part of the process.

I've had many years of classroom experience, teaching writing every year in first, second, third, fourth, fifth, and sixth

My Pedagogical Foundations

- Joy
- Engagement
- Trust
- Sense-Making
- Authenticity
- Choice
- Autonomy
- Agency
- Intentionality
- Honesty
- Reflection
- Communication
- Connection
- Culturally and Linguistically Sustaining Practices
- Whole Child, Asset-Based Instruction

grades. I've had daily opportunities to make a whole bunch of mistakes (or "learning opportunities" as a former fifth grader once called them) and have learned alongside hundreds and hundreds of writers in the elementary grades. I continue to learn and revise my thinking every single day. I care deeply about young people and have learned the power of listening to the voices of all children in my classrooms over the years. My work is grounded in listening to and elevating those young voices as they learn to become storytellers and poets and graphic novelists and historians and nonfiction fanatics and activists who believe their words have power and purpose.

When the children in our classroom have an audience and a purpose for their writing, their engagement and commitment soar.

You're invited to step inside our classroom and witness the joy and the messiness and the ideas that, over the years, seem to work with lots of groups of children.

Throughout this piece, you will find a variety of ways to honor and showcase writers' voices. When the children in our classroom have an audience and a purpose for their writing, their engagement and commitment soar. They come to believe that their words (oral and written) have power to incite action, create emotion, provide entertainment and information, push back on stereotypes, create change, and build a better world.

I reject the idea that a child's writing experience in school should be one that focuses solely on correcting all that's "not conventional" with a piece—correcting spelling and grammar and punctuation and handwriting and sentence structure and organization and and and . . . until young writers feel defeated before they even start. Yes, that work is important in certain parts of the process. However, the work of a writer and the identity of a writer and the dreams and purposes of a writer are far greater and more significant than the limiting definition of what school has defined as "proficient."

I also recognize that many of you, like myself, have taught or are teaching in schools with strict mandates and guide-

lines, with scripts and programs. I, too, teach with these pressures and mandates, and I have standards and guidelines to meet. In this piece I hope to share time-tested routines and ways to honor your beliefs and pedagogy while at the same time making space as you work under the state-, district-, or schoolwide mandates teachers so often face.

What Does This Look Like in Practice?

I'll begin by sharing how I design a space conducive to growing writers who not only write with purpose and power but who love the work they do each day. We'll dig into ways to build writing routines and community in those first weeks of school and how to keep the momentum and learning going week after week after week. We'll explore ways to intentionally teach talking and listening to build writer identity and independence. While learning from the young writers I sit alongside each day, I'll share how I discover and use mentor texts that give writers a sense and a vision of what's possible in their own work, and we'll even discover that classmates can become writing mentors as well! I'll share ways we can honor and showcase writers' voices throughout the entire process. We'll slow down to honor even the tiniest details and writerly habits, looking at all students' work through an asset lens and celebrating the small (and the big) growth writers make. Finally, we'll talk about how to not give up or give in to your beliefs in the midst of scripted curriculum and mandates from outside the classroom.

With a disposition of inquiry and celebration, let's journey together through the first nine weeks of school with a group of growing writers.

How Do I Design a Classroom Space for Writers?

Children deserve to live their lives believing that school is a place where they can and do live joyfully. They deserve to have daily opportunities to think, talk, write, read, and grow in a space that honors their humanity, their voices, and their freedom. They deserve to authentically engage in daily practices that will give them the skills to lead lives as agentive, collaborative, productive, creative, confident, world-bettering people. To create opportunities like these in school, I must first design a classroom space that speaks to and honors these beliefs about children.

In *Culturally Responsive Teaching and the Brain: Promoting Authentic Engagement and Rigor among Culturally and Linguistically Diverse Students* (2015), Zaretta Hammond talks about the power of creating a space for children to learn and build their intellectual capacity. "We should not underestimate the power of the classroom community to support dependent learners move toward more independent learning. The feeling tone and structure of a welcoming classroom can help students enter and maintain a state of relaxed alertness that lays the foundation for authentic engagement" (p. 193).

The agency this approach affords students is discussed in NCTE's *The Students' Right to Write* position statement (2026): "In defending students' right to write, we defend their right to think expansively, to question freely, and to use writing as a tool for truth-telling, creativity, and justice throughout their lives in a democratic society."

Matching Your Beliefs to Classroom Design

IF I BELIEVE that building community is at the heart of all the work we will do, I need to create a space where we can gather as a community of learners to think, read, write, talk, problem solve, and celebrate our learning.

IF I BELIEVE that all children learn best when they're comfortable and have choice in seating and work spaces, I need to intentionally create spaces where children can choose the types of seating arrangements or gathering areas in which they engage in productive learning, conversation, and creation.

IF I BELIEVE that children become stronger writers by studying authors, writing structures, crafting techniques, and a variety of genres, I need to build a classroom library that facilitates and welcomes that active reading and studying of mentor texts.

IF I BELIEVE that young writers should be using the tools that published writers use to create their pieces, I need to set up spaces in the room filled with those same tools for storytelling, writing, and illustrating work.

IF I BELIEVE in creating a setting that demonstrates my convictions about power structures, autonomy, and agency, I need to ensure that my classroom becomes *our* classroom. I am intentional about redefining what it means to share space and materials with all learners. The "teacher area" becomes low profile and is never off limits to students during our writing, reading, and creating times.

IF I BELIEVE that the environment, the classroom itself, is the third teacher, I need to ensure that lighting, room colors, design, and decorative touches enhance rather than inhibit student engagement and focus.

Setting Up the Environment for Writers

The large area rug is the center of gravity in our classroom. It's the space we gather to learn, talk, share, laugh, and wrestle with ideas. It's the place where community comes to life, and from it learners launch (multiple times a day) into meaningful reading and writing work. This place is our watering hole, our place to be one, and a place to celebrate so much of the work we do together. I teach focus lessons here, and the kids share their writing here every day. We solve problems here. We learn how to talk to each other here. We make new friends here. And we first learn that our voices and ideas matter here.

The area rug has become a nonnegotiable piece of the classroom design. Once I have the area rug, the design elements of the room grow from it . . . colors and textures and furniture and room organization are built around that rug so that I can center children in all the work I do.

Seating and Workspace Choices

I've filled my classroom with tables, small benches, rugs, and pillows instead of desks. This kind of furniture facilitates the kind of talk, the kind of writing and reading discourse I will teach and encourage. It also sends a message to writers that I value their differences and needs as writers and people. I don't do my best work sitting at a desk all day, so why should children be any different? I will not be standing front and center to deliver lectures but will be pulling up alongside a writer to listen in, confer, and nudge them forward in their writing work each day. This kind of space feels comfortable and more like a home, a library, or a coffee shop—places that writers tend to choose to work rather than in a sterile room with desks in rows.

In the room, you'll find that some tables are round seating or standing height while

others are low to the ground and rectangular. Benches, stools, and baskets of clipboards are placed strategically throughout the room and send a gentle message to a writer to pull up a seat and settle in to work. Chairs are also spaced along a long countertop near the windows. This gives writers the opportunity to choose a place that works best for them, whether it be a straight-back chair and a flat workspace, a quiet area on a pillow in the corner, a table space with a window view, or a spot on the big rug for a middle-of-the-room energy. In all parts of the room, these work spaces are surrounded by books. These books will be the ones the kids will fall in love with . . . the ones that will become friends, mentors, and quiet coaches for their writing work in the year ahead.

Writing Material and Supply Areas

Most writing supplies are located in one main area of the classroom (both on the countertop and organized in cabinets above the counter), and I spend the first month of school introducing the types of supplies that writers might use to draft, edit, revise, or publish a piece. Children quickly begin to see that I value their work as writers, and they can expect to use the exact tools that "real" writers use on a daily basis. It's important to help students understand the use and purpose of each of these tools so they can then make decisions about the best materials for where they are in their process as a writer. For example, a writer working on an initial idea or draft in their notebook or folder might need blank paper and a few pencils but won't need Sharpie markers or watercolors at this point in their process. However, when it's time to publish and showcase the writer's final piece, it's time to bring out the fancy markers and paints! Our writing supply area evolves

Supply caddies with writing supplies are located on every table in the classroom.

as our writing studies and understanding of the purpose of each writing tool grows throughout the year. Students see what's possible with the tools at their fingertips, and they use these materials with eagerness and care each day because I've taught them how to use the materials and trusted them to use the materials and tools wisely and well.

In addition to the main writing supply counter area, I've chosen to create separate storage spaces for materials and supplies around the room. Because I believe that "students have a right to decision-making in their creativity, voice, and expression of ideas" (from NCTE's *The Students' Right to Write* position statement, 2026), I believe part of that decision-making comes from having choices about the kinds of supplies and materials they will choose to write and create with each day. I've found that this type of organization (creating multiple areas for writing materials and supplies) helps alleviate congested areas where all writers gather at once so that we have smooth and timely transitions from one block of time to the next. These strategic supply areas also give me ways to help students (and myself) stay organized and find the materials we need quickly and easily. I don't have separate desks in my classroom this year, so each table area has one community supply box. At the beginning of the year, I teach the children how to store materials properly and then the Writing Team or the Folders, Paper, and Notebooks Team (classroom teams that rotate every two weeks) take charge of keeping the areas organized and free of clutter for the rest of the year.

Classroom Library Organization and Arrangement

In the classroom library, I've designated two areas for books that can be mentors for writers during each study. In the photo below is one of those shelves that showcases different poetry books we're using to begin our first poetry genre study. Books like *Hip Hop Speaks to Children* (2008), edited by Nikki Giovanni, immediately invite writers in to see that poetry has a rhythm and is much like the music they listen to every day, featuring contributions from artists in both realms, from Langston Hughes and Maya Angelou to Queen Latifah and Tupac Shakur. Sitting right next to Giovanni is Rajani LaRocca's *Your One and Only Heart* (2023), one for my science lovers to explore how to weave science and nonfiction information into their own poetry. Charles Waters and Irene Latham's *Dictionary for A Better World: Poems, Quotes, and Anecdotes from A to Z* (2020) gives an alphabetic structure and teaches us all kinds of lessons with words for a better world, from acceptance to zest.

The other "reading-for-writing" facing-out shelf is located across the room. These two shelves are located on opposite sides of the classroom, strategically placed between the rest of the library so that students become comfortable with reading for different purposes at different times—either reading for pleasure and enjoyment in independent reading, reading to learn new information, reading to teach someone something, or reading to learn the craft and structures of a particular genre of writing.

Bookshelves face out with beginning-of-the-year mentor texts.

Classroom library shelves can be dedicated to serve different purposes.

These two special facing-out bookshelves were built to showcase the covers of books so that children are drawn to these spaces and have easy access to titles they may need for writing and studying a specific genre, craft, structure, or idea about writing. These shelves are home to mentor texts, exemplifying the genre or kind of writing we are studying at a particular time of the year.

At the beginning of the year, I might use one shelf to highlight a variety of picturebooks, simply giving writers ideas for writing topics or ways to structure a piece of writing. We might use another shelf to house all our favorite poetry books and ones we're learning from and trying to emulate in our own writing. (I'll delve more deeply into the collection and my decisions about choosing mentor texts in a later section.)

In addition to these shelves, I've intentionally organized books in different locations for easy access so that students can find books they either want to read or study as a writing mentor.

The photograph at the top of this page shows one of those low, facing-out bookshelves designated for writing mentors and also highlights a section of the classroom library for readers. You can see books by Christian Robinson, books that we used for our writing self-portrait project that I'll talk about in later sections. The shelf on the left is designated for book baskets for author investigations or extra texts we're using during writing time but need a place

Series books with student-created labels

to store temporarily. The tall bookshelf is designed for independent reading books, with both novels and picturebooks alphabetized by title. For the children and me, alphabetizing by title is easier when trying to locate a particular book. I've noticed that children remember titles easily, so this is why I don't organize books by the author's last name. This is just one section of the classroom library, but it shows how books of all types and for all purposes are organized in a single area.

> Even making decisions with the children about classroom library organization and labeling the bookshelves for easy access shows children that their writing, their creativity, their opinions, and their voices matter.

Even making decisions with the children about classroom library organization and labeling the bookshelves for easy access shows children that their writing, their creativity, their opinions, and their voices matter.

As always, keeping my beliefs about children and how they learn at the forefront of my mind helps me create a clear vision for the classroom environment I hope to create each year. With children at the center of each decision—from furniture and supply choices to room arrangement to color scheme and lighting, I'm always able to stay true to a classroom design that works for and supports young writers and readers.

Easy Design Moves That Don't Break the Bank

Over the years, I've learned how to make use of materials and furniture that were in my classroom before I arrived. When I was just starting as a teacher, I wondered how I would ever be able to create (and afford) the furniture and materials I wanted for my students. I do recognize and still experience many years where there just aren't funds in my bank account (or my school budget) to purchase that area rug or any special touches that make the classroom feel like home.

Here are ways that I've been able to stay true to my beliefs about classroom setup and design without spending a ton of money in the process.

Places to regularly visit for potential classroom treasures:

- Get to know your neighborhood yard sales, estate sales, and thrift stores for rugs, decor, and furniture for a fraction of the cost of brand-new items.
- Big box or discount stores that carry unbound rugs or rug remnants will many times make donations to schools or classrooms.
- Every summer, I do a little crafting project using old lampshades. I de-coupage old or torn book covers onto the shades and paint the bases of old lamps to freshen the look.

Ways to make old furniture and storage materials look like brand new:

- Spray paint that adheres to plastic has been a lifesaver in reusing boxes and bins for storage year after year
- A can of paint can do wonders to freshen up furniture or change the look of a classroom from year to year.

If You Want to Learn More about Classroom Setup and Design...

Classroom Design for Student Agency: Create Spaces to Empower Young Readers and Writers, Lynsey Burkins and Franki Sibberson (2023)

Rooted in Joy: Creating a Classroom Culture of Equity, Belonging, and Joy, Deonna Smith, Jossey-Bass (2023)

How Do I Launch Writing and Build Community?

As I begin a writing year with children, before I start with any other goals or plans, I first ask the children what they need from me. I care about how they think and what they say. Their voices and ideas matter to me above all else. In *Writing Reimagined: Bridging Critical Theories and Pedagogical Practices in the Elementary Classroom* (Yang & Cline, 2026), Katie Peachie and Crystal Chen Lee contribute the piece "Identity at the Core: Student Identities and Writing Instruction in the Elementary Classroom." In it they say, "Honoring and valuing students' multiple identities—and acting in ways that make this commitment visible—is at the heart of a critical and humanizing approach to writing instruction. Identity matters. We need to know our students and create space for them to show up fully, as their whole selves" (p. 26).

I know we have curriculum to teach and standards to meet and goals to reach, but curricula and standards and goals mean nothing to children until they know that their voices and identities are at the center of it all. Meeting the standards and reaching grade-level benchmarks become collaborative (not just the work for the teacher) when children know we are invested in and choose to first honor their ideas and their thinking.

Two questions I ask the first week of school help set the tone for the kind of writing classroom I want for a group of students each year:

1. What do you need from your teacher?

2. What do you need from your classmates?

The answers I get are never about needing special teaching in a particular content area or in preparation for a standardized test. I don't think I've ever had a student say, "I need you to teach me how to get ready for the ACAP test in April" or "I am looking to meet the fourth-grade ELA standard #30 so that I can be successful at text-dependent writing—I need lots of lessons about how to do that."

Instead, I get answers about "heart care." Kids want to feel happy, calm, safe, valued, respected, appreciated, listened to, celebrated. . . . They ask these same things of their classmates. Yes, the answers are about basic human needs, but shouldn't our teaching, no matter what, be about seeing our students in their full humanity and building every ounce of work together from that foundation?

It always reminds me that students who feel seen and heard and valued are always more engaged and receptive to our teaching and feedback if those basic needs are not just being met but are put first in our work. No lesson plan ever asks for heart care, but our writers ask for and deserve it every single time. And in time, once we attend first (and always) to their hearts, we will find writers and readers who actually grow far beyond what's expected from a state mandated standard or a standardized test.

I always like to say my job is to put myself out of a job . . . to make sure my students are doing the heavy lifting instead of me. What are some ways I help students start to take ownership for the work in our classroom space every day?

Classroom Teams

Classroom Teams have become a way to launch a community of agentive learners. In the first weeks of school, I ask the kids to brainstorm things that need "getting done" or "taken care of" in the classroom. The word *job* felt too heavy to them, so one group said we should call these groups *teams* . . . because teams work together for the good of many to get something accomplished. So, Classroom Teams were born. We spend time talking as a whole class and in partnerships about what each team might do, and the children figure out what needs to be done and create bulleted lists of the job descriptions. These are 100 percent kid created, and as much as I want my voice in this, it's critical to give the children the space and autonomy to make these decisions. This work is a form of honoring their identities and their voices early on without fear of censorship from the adult in the room. They first start with brainstorming about the kinds of tasks that need to be accomplished in the room on a daily basis.

For example, we have lots of lamps in the room, and someone has to be responsible for plugging/unplugging or turning lamps on and off every day. The table writing supply caddies have lots of writing materials that are organized in a particular way and need to stay organized for easy access and use. Daily routines like lunch count and attendance have to be taken every morning, and someone needs to be responsible for that. Once they've brainstormed their ideas, they make decisions about who might want to be the founding members of the team and launch this work for the rest of the class. We take time to

The set of Teams panels (left) and a detailed look at the responsibilities and roster for the FPN (Folders, Paper, and Notebooks) Team (right)

discuss and come to a consensus that everyone can agree on, and every child finds their place on a team. (Sometimes we have to draw names at first when there are highly sought-after teams.)

After teams are solidified, the founding members design, list job descriptions, and name the team on a poster to hang in the classroom for the year. Teams rotate every two weeks. Every year the teams are a bit different. Once we make a list of all the tasks that need accomplishing, we think about how we might group these tasks. For example, the children decide that the "writing supply team" is responsible for making sure the whole-class writing supply area is organized and table caddies have the writing tools they need. The Tech Team is in charge of taking lunch count on the computer, showing announcement slides, and helping anyone with Chromebook issues. The FPN Team passes out and picks up/organizes folders, papers, and notebooks when needed. As these teams are created, the class brainstorms descriptions for the work each team will do.

Prince works on the Bookkeepers Team.

Brandt works on the Lunch Team.

Meyer works on the Lamps and Pillows Team.

The teams rotate on a twice-monthly basis, so every two weeks, students choose their top three team choices, and I use their choices to make the teams (two to three students per team) for the next two weeks. The class decided that it's important to choose a different team every two weeks until each person has had the opportunity to work on every team. The class felt this was a fair way for all students to try out each team and be responsible for every part of ensuring our daily writing time (and whole classroom) runs smoothly.

Part of building community is establishing ways for the children to be the decision makers and co-creators of as much of the work of the classroom as possible.

The Tech Team is in charge of taking the lunch count and showing the morning announcement slides, along with being tech support for anyone with Chromebook or classroom tech tool challenges and questions.

Being in charge of their own Classroom Teams sends the message that they have decision-making power and can get things accomplished as a community. Every part of what we do contributes to community building for student agency. Everything from having a group of kids managing the lunch choices and lunch count to turning the lamps and lights on/off to returning books to their proper places in the classroom library are ways to teach independence and responsibility and to foster autonomy and agency for even bigger work to come. The teams we create as a class are one way to give all students daily opportunities to take the lead in our learning and make sure that necessary routines run smoothly to make our learning possible.

Ellis stocks pencils for the Writers Team.

Anthony passes out notebooks as part of the FPN team.

Launching Writing

Launching writing begins with all children seeing themselves as writers and actually believing it. You can't create a community of writers with people who only see writing as a task to be graded and sent home in a folder. Writers need a place that honors their home languages, their lived experiences, both in and out of school, and multiple ways to represent their ideas, whether it be through oral storytelling, collecting materials for journaling, drawing, translanguaging, or a mixture of all. The children we teach deserve to experience and create and wrestle with ideas just as "real" writers do. What does that look like in an elementary classroom? First, we must give children the tools that writers use, honor and celebrate what they bring to our classrooms, and trust them to make choices in how to use those tools and materials.

"You are no longer Ben . . . you are *Ben, the Writer*. You are no longer Elliott . . . you are *Elliott, the Writer*. You are no longer Isabella . . . you are *Isabella, the Writer*." You'll hear me declare this truth over every student in the classroom as they receive their first writer's notebook.

There's nothing special about this notebook. It's a black and white marble composition notebook—a 99-cent notebook from the local office supply store that will become a storehouse for ideas. A treasure chest of sorts. What transforms the notebook from "plain ole notebook" to a writing identity treasure chest is the young writer who now owns the notebook. It's a personal space to write and sketch and collect photos and artifacts and ideas....a garden to nurture and grow the seeds that will become poems and stories and nonfiction pieces in the days and weeks to come. It's personal. It's powerful. It's a place to bring what matters in their lives to the forefront of the writing work we'll do—not something from a script or a test or a teacher created assignment.

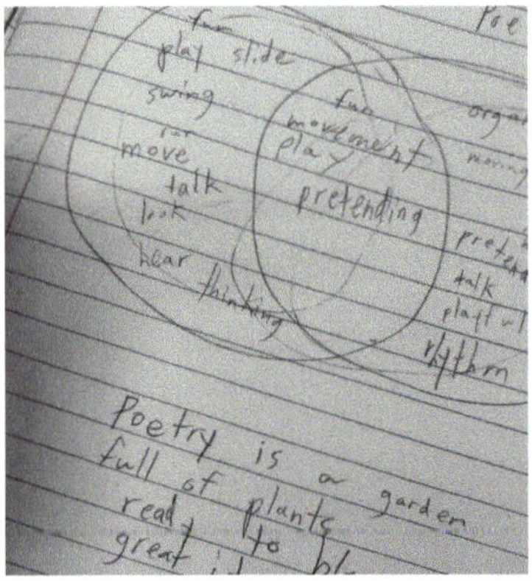

This year, the children decided to organize their writer's notebooks in interesting ways . . . a section for

Writer's notebook covers designed by students

ideas, notes, sketches, photos, and drafts, a section for vocabulary collecting, a "100 Things about Me as a Writer" section (which I'll talk about more later), and a section for writing conference notes. Vocabulary collecting has been especially popular this year with these writers. Revising poetry drafts with figurative language, paying close attention to interesting and unknown words during read aloud, and student-driven morphology and spelling investigations have all emerged from these lists of words in the writer's notebook.

When children feel and believe that they are living daily in a place where their lives inside and outside the classroom are honored and celebrated, beautiful work happens. The writer's notebook is a foundational tool for purposes not constrained by the rules of school but brought forth into the classroom to unleash multiple ways to represent and celebrate the identities of every child.

Self-Portraits

From day one, my goal is to lift, honor, and showcase the voices and the work of writers and highlight the good stuff every chance I get. Oral storytelling is a big part of our work as writers, and in the first few weeks of school, getting the children to talk about the stories of their lives is the first step in honoring their voices. Sharing their histories and identities by creating the self-portrait collage is a great way to honor each writer/storyteller/artist's identity while also publishing a piece that becomes a springboard for more talk and writing and celebration.

Many times we think of "writing" work as only putting words on paper for an audience to read. However, building community with a group of students and igniting a love of writing needs to first begin with storytelling and art centered around the identities of the children who will soon see themselves and authors and illustrators. Who am I as a unique person, an independent thinker, a curious learner . . . and an agentive writer? I want the learners who enter my classroom to first believe that their unique gifts, backgrounds, cultures, and identities are fertile soil for developing their own ideas for writing. One way we capture the beauty of the humans who inhabit the learning space we create together is by first creating self-portrait collages.

With the self-portraits, my goal is first to help the learners in my classroom come to understand that our definition of writing is composing that is multi-dimensional. We will share our ideas, passions, voices, and lives . . . in different modes . . . with different tools . . . with different processes . . . and for different purposes. Writing is multimodal, and our composing sometimes comes through storytelling, building, or art, and our first published piece of writing becomes a permanent piece of artwork that hangs in our classroom to ignite and inspire future writing ideas. Before we hang the self-portraits, students share them with classmates and we talk about ways these pieces will become a springboard for future writing ideas and projects.

This year's self-portrait collages were inspired by the style of Christian Robinson.

Mariano shares the "loves" in his life—family, dogs, alligators, sports teams and players. His religion and family are central to his linguistic identity, and he's proud to use both English and Spanish fluently to give life to who he is. When he shared his self-portrait with the class, we learned that he was also eager to help us speak and translate from Spanish, his home language, to English, recognizing that I am not the sole bearer of knowledge and that we celebrate many ways of knowing and communicating together. Mariano uses bilingual texts from our classroom to teach his peers how to speak his language and create his own multilingual texts. From Mariano we will soon learn the power of translanguaging and writing bilingually, as he is eager to speak, storytell, and write using his entire language repertoire. The self-portrait conversation ignited this work and deepened my understanding of Mariano.

Mariano's self-portrait

Mariano and Christopher read *Tíos and Primos* (2025), by Jacqueline Alcántara, a book written in both English and Spanish about a little girl meeting more relatives than she can count and wondering how she will communicate with them if she can't speak their language.

Malea is known as the classroom artist and regularly collaborates with her classmates.

Malea is a seamstress, designer, knitter, and gifted artist. A self-proclaimed "mama's baby," messy artist, bird lover, and Auburn fan, she wasn't afraid to tell me she was bored easily and proudly announced that to anyone who read the description around her portrait. Her classmates have named her "our artist," and she regularly collaborates as illustrator with many of her classmates on co-created pieces of writing. Her words ring true with honesty, without fear of being censored but instead being celebrated, and she recognizes that her artwork is a central part of her writing process.

Malea's self-portrait

Anthony doesn't like writing because the physical act of putting pencil to paper is hard. He isn't afraid to tell me and isn't afraid to say it's hard. However, his self-portrait showcases that he's strong, a leader, helpful . . . and a sports, country music, and puzzle fan! He also loves talking about books and sharing what he's learning from those books with friends. These are the strengths we focus on from the very beginning so that he can showcase his passions and powerful, confident identity. I then direct him to other ways to share his voice and ideas, not just with paper and pencil . . . digital storytelling with audio

Anthony's self-portrait

Anthony goes beyond pen and paper to share his ideas.

recording tools, text-to-speech apps, lots of opportunities to talk and share, shifting his original thought that he's not a writer into someone who sees multiple opportunities to communicate his ideas and his voice to an audience of readers and listeners.

Where Do Writers Get Ideas?

"I don't know what to write about." "I don't have anything to write." "I can't think of anything to say."

Have you ever heard your students make these comments? I can't count the number of times! It's important that students feel safe to discuss struggling with and disliking writing. However, it's also important to help students see what I see. As I pull up alongside students, together, we work to look through an asset lens for all the ways our students bring expertise into the classroom and all the ways and places that writers get ideas.

At the beginning of each year, I've learned to be intentional about spending time helping students name and highlight

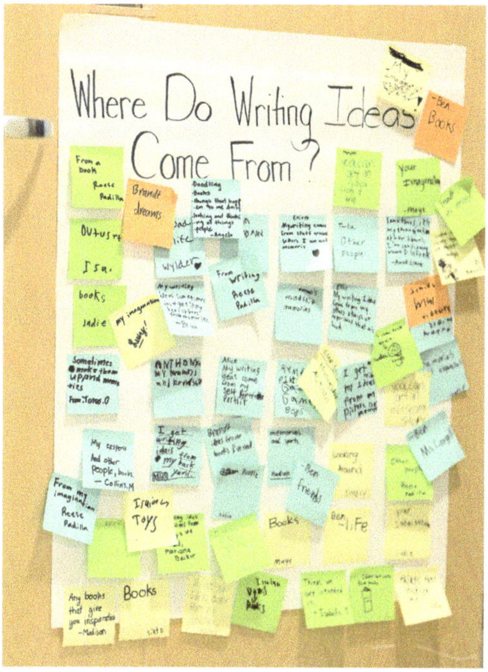

A "Where Do Writing Ideas Come From" chart from the beginning of the school year

the possibilities for getting writing ideas so that these "I can't" statements evaporate and become replaced with "What might I try today in my writing?" or "I think I'll work on this idea first and save this one for another time," or "This seems like a great idea that could become a graphic novel," or "I think we could make a two-voice poem using this idea!" "I might draw for a while and then talk about my story to my partner." "I might read and gather ideas in my notebook." "I'm going to use the voice recorder to capture my story first."

We begin to build a chart with student ideas about how they generate writing ideas and refer back to that chart anytime a writer is "stuck" with "nothing to write about." The list grows and changes throughout the year, and I've found that it's important to photograph and keep track of the changes in the chart as the year moves on. It's a fantastic reflection tool for the students so they see how their thinking grows and changes as they grow and change as writers and readers.

How Can I Help Chart?

The children need to see themselves as

Where Do Writing Ideas Come From?
My memories and knowledge (Anthony S.)
Books (Jadie)
My imagination (Lucille)
My friends (Ben)
Outside (Isaiah)
Things that interest me (Lou)
Looking around (Emory)
My writing ideas come from my self-portrait (Alice)
I think them up (a.k.a make them up!) (Colton)
Life (Wylder)
Dreams (Brandt)
From writing! (Reese)

co-teachers in the classroom, as people who have the ability to share their knowledge, gifts, and understandings with fellow classmates. I want this for the students so that they will develop a sense of agency and independence and not rely on me for all decision making in the classroom. It frees up my teaching space as well, giving me one-on-one time with each student while also watching peer-to-peer teaching, coaching, and support happen among students while I'm busy teaching elsewhere in the room.

Over the first month of school, the children begin to learn about each other and quickly come to know who's good at what: the artists, the organizers, the people who are great at loading the stapler and finding the perfect color choices in the marker boxes. Nothing is off limits for the "How Can I Help?" chart because we all need help with something, and it's our opportunity to name all the "good somethings" we bring to this

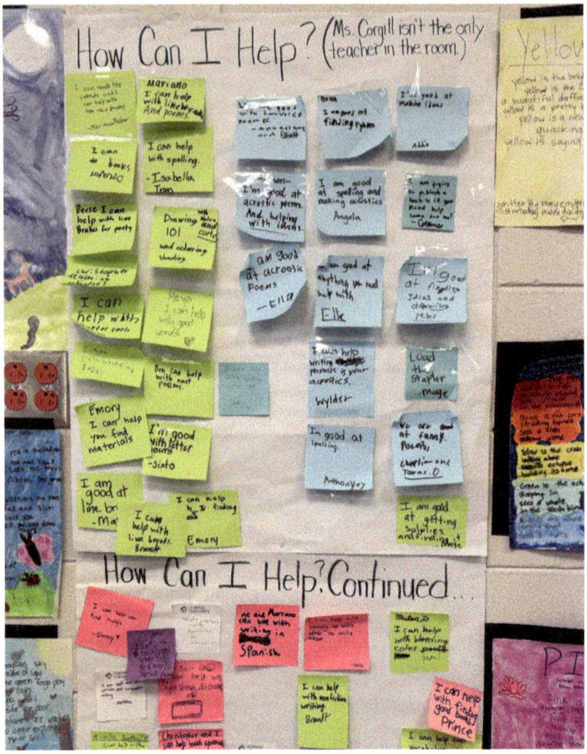

classroom and this writing work every day. From watching and listening closely to my students, I'm able to remind those children who don't see their inherent gifts and talents as something that might fit on a "How Can I Help?" chart, so I name talents to shift that perspective. It's a conscious shift in thinking to a disposition of inquiry and curiosity, a disposition and learning stance that gets us to the root of the "I don't have anything to offer" feelings and pushes me to bring student brilliance to the forefront of our work.

Learners might need reminding that helping classmates find materials in the room is a strength and a gift. Finding a book that's hidden in the room is a gift for someone who just can't seem to find what they're looking for at the moment. Mixing the right amount of water with tempera paint is a gift. Seeing and naming student gifts and talents is the goal—and then watching them recognize and use those gifts and talents for others is a way to build agency, joy, and independence.

Students add their expertise to the chart when ready, and then other students can access their help when needed by reading the chart and finding the expert in the room.

Building a strong classroom community hinges on one big idea: **All voices and identities are valued and celebrated in this classroom.** Everyone has something to offer—an area of expertise, a passion, a strength, an inherent gift, an untapped talent, a challenge that becomes a success story, an ability to offer support, a heart to bring out the best in others, a vision for who we can become as a group of learners. The community we build is only as strong as the people who make up the community, and it is a privilege to learn, work alongside, and grow communities of writers and learners each year. Listen to and honor the voices of the writers in your care. The knowledge and wisdom of children will never let you down.

How Can I Help?

Early Year

I can help you find materials. (Emory)

I can help with spelling. (Isabella)

Drawing 101, coloring, and shading (Malea)

Reading drafts! (Christopher)

I can help with good words. (Meyer)

After Nine Weeks of Writing

I am really good at starting a story or a paragraph. (Wylder)

I can help with slideshows and documents . . . and I am good with technology when things go away or pop up. (Ben)

Christopher and I can help teach Spanish to write. (Mariano)

I'm good at searching things on the computer. (Ella)

I can spell a lot of words and computer writing. (Mariana)

I can help make poems. (Jadie)

I can write in Ukrainian and Russian. (Taras)

Notice how the "How Can I Help?" chart has evolved over the first nine weeks of school.

If You Want to Learn More about Building a Classroom Community...

Lessons in Community: A Teacher's Guide to Imagining Classroom Management and Social-Emotional Learning by Mari Dean (2025)

Writing Reimagined: Bridging Critical Theories and Pedagogical Practices in Elementary Classrooms by Grace Y. Yang and Sonia M. Kline (2026)

How Do I Create Daily Routines That Ignite and Sustain Writing Engagement?

Launching the workshop with groups of writers takes a commitment to manageable, daily routines that may seem too simple to add up to much at first glance. How could just giving kids time to write each day do much for their growth? What's so special about making daily, intentional time for students to share their writing? Why trust a simple focus lesson to ignite a collective enthusiasm around one type of writing?

I've been doing this work for over 30 years, and time after time, year after year, I've witnessed the power of how these simple, intentional routines become the foundation for each group of writers and help us build a strong classroom community.

The three overarching parts of the writing workshop are (1) focus lesson, (2) independent (or collaborative) writing and conferring (these parts happen simultaneously), and (3) share.

Focus Lesson

What happens in a focus lesson? These lessons begin our writing work each day, and one small part of our process as writers is the focus. I start all lessons with a question to get students thinking about what would work best for us as a class, not just for me, their teacher. It shifts the stance from the teacher telling students what to do to learners engaging in plans and solutions.

At the beginning of the year, as I launch writing time with students, focus lessons might center on a new classroom writing routine (how to get your writing materials, choose an independent work space, and begin writing).

Something as simple as learning how to locate and use the writing materials in the classroom becomes a series of focus lessons at the beginning of the year. These types of focus lessons set the stage for lessons centered on specific writing skills and craft as the year progresses.

Focus Lesson Prompts to Engage Students in Planning

Supplies

- How might we organize the supplies we use every day so that everyone has easy access?
- What would it do for you as writers if we had these supplies located in multiple spots in the room?
- How might it make our transition from lesson to writing time smoother and more efficient?
- What do we do about materials we don't use every day but need from time to time in the writing process?
- How do we clean up and prepare these spaces for tomorrow's work when we're finished writing for the day?

Writing Conferences (Both Teacher and Peer)

- When you have a question, need support, or want someone to listen to your writing, that's a signal you might need a writing conference. Let's talk about some ways we can schedule and sign up for writing conferences.
- If I'm busy meeting with a student or a group, what might you do to get your question answered or to get help with your writing?
- What kinds of conferences are most helpful to you at certain times during your process? (More on the types of conferences later in this section.)

Seating Spaces for Work

- Why are seating spaces and specific work areas important for writers?
- Talk to your partner about the spaces in the room where you work best when writing and why those spaces work for you.
- How might we handle the issue of multiple people wanting to sit at the low table with cushions during writing time?
- What should the seating spaces look like at the end of writing time so we're ready to move on to other work?

Papers and Notebooks

- How might we quickly pass out notebooks and folders so that writers can begin work in a timely manner?
- Why might it be important for us to date every piece of writing we attempt this year and make that a non-negotiable?
- What happens when you're ready to start a draft after working on ideas for a while in your writer's notebook?
- How do we keep the folders, notebooks, and paper organized so everyone can find their materials when needed?

Mentor Texts

- Where might you go in the room to find a book that can teach you something about writing?
- Could you and your partner spend some time reading and discovering new ideas about this genre? Would you be willing to share your discoveries with the class?
- What poetry book that we've read (or any genre you're studying could fit here) might demonstrate how you could structure your piece of writing?

Writing Conferences

Conferring is a daily, powerful routine, a time to honor the writer's voice and ideas and give that writer the time they crave with me, their teacher. Writers deserve daily constructive feedback, and conferring is at the heart of learning to give and receive feedback, to nudge writing forward. Where does the content for each conference come from? How do I plan for conferring?

In Stella Villalba's book, *Tell Me More: Conferring with Artists, Writers, and Storytellers* (2026), she reminds us that "teaching and learning are rooted in collectivist practices. One way we are truly going to grow as a community of learners is by honoring the voices of children, including them in the co-creation of learning and meaning" (p. 4).

My teaching, learning, and conferring with children is rooted in what we learn together. Their lives and their questions guide my planning and are at the forefront of my conferring.

I listen closely to student conversations and pore over their folders full of illustrations and entries and drafts. Because I listen to the children in my classroom and read their writing frequently, I have teaching material at my fingertips. Students know this after I've read pieces in their folders or entries in their writer's notebook. I see that a conference might lift the level of that work or push the writer to think in a way that supports their writing process or product. They come to expect this routine and are eager to sit alongside me and chat about the writing work they've done. As we create a routine of daily conferring, students come to realize that there are different purposes for wanting or needing a conference.

Conferring can take on different forms each day, from one-on-one to small group to peer conferring, and it's these moments with writers that evolve and develop over the course of the year. We decide as a class when we need one-on-one time, time to confer with classmates, or just time for classmates to chat with one another about their writing.

- Do you need a "listen and celebrate" conference?
- Do you need a "next steps with mentor texts" conference?
- Do you need a "new tools and techniques" conference?

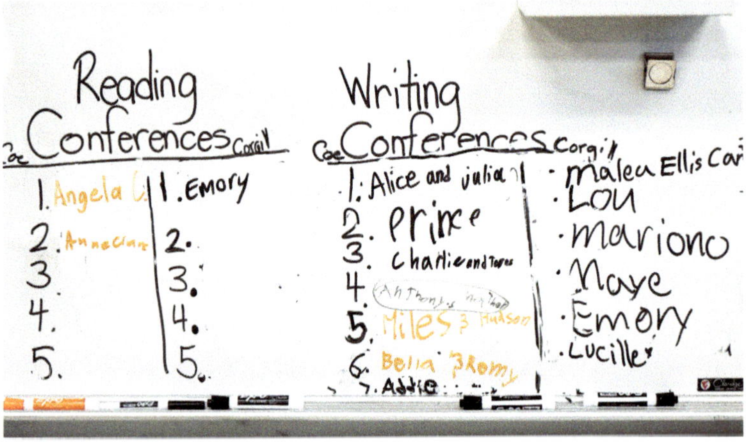

Conference sign-ups on the dry-erase board

- Do you need a "prep for writing share" conference?

We might spend several days listing and defining the types of conferences students might need or want so that they become central to the decision making about when and why to meet with me or a peer. I don't want my conferring to be just a list of names to check off so that I can say I've met with a student.

In the classroom I also have a sign-up spot on the dry-erase board for students who know they need to talk to me or who have questions about their writing or their process. Students sign up to meet with me as needed, and I move to each student in the order they sign up. Many days, this responsive conferring takes the place of my planned conferences because responding to student needs and requests takes priority.

Alice shares her poem with me.

Conferences to Listen and Celebrate

Sometimes I might just stop to listen in on the progress a writer is making, and in this case, Alice is sharing the beginning draft of a two-voice poem she and Julia are working on. She just wanted me to listen in and celebrate with her.

Conferences to Offer or Introduce New Tools

Sometimes conferences are quick "how-to" opportunities with writers. In this conference, I'm showing Anthony how to upload a piece of writing he's audio recorded so he can listen and then transcribe what he's written. This is a strategy I might use for writers who are more comfortable telling their stories first and then making a place to keep them so they can transcribe them later if needed.

Anthony and I talk about audio recording/listening.

Conferences to Suggest Next Steps or Mentor Texts When Writers Are Stuck

I show Mariano part of the book that's written in two languages.

Sometimes I might share observation notes with writers during a conference to make next steps or share mentor texts to support those next moves the writer might make. In this conference, I'm talking with Mariano and sharing the mentor text *Delicious: Poems Celebrating Street Food around the World* by Julie Larios (2021). This is a book he might use as he and his friend Christopher co-create a poem in Spanish, the language both he and Christopher speak at home with their families. They are both fluent Spanish and English speakers and are excited to try writing in both languages to share and teach the class what they're passionate about, what they're learning, and what they already know!

Many times, our conferences turn into matchmaker moments, like the one above with Mariano, when I'm able to match the writer with the type of mentor text they're trying to write.

Christopher and Mariano proudly share their Al-Nassr professional soccer acrostic poem. Our writing time becomes their time to share a love of their favorite soccer team and player, Cristiano Ronaldo, and celebrate their bilingualism (with illustrating and watercolor expertise from their classmate Malea).

I share a mentor text with Colton that matches his writing interest.

In one particular conference, Colton, who's obsessed with graphic novels, wanted to try to write one of his own, but he couldn't figure out how to keep working on poetry while also writing a graphic novel, so I shared the book *Poetry Comics* by Grant Snider (2024) with him, a book written as a collection of poems in graphic novel style. This is why being a reader and being intentional about knowing books of all types and genres is critical to the teaching of writing. This process is ongoing, and it's probably one of the most important elements of my professional growth over the years. We'll talk more about how I learn about and study books as models for writing in the "Mentor Texts" section.

I can typically meet with three to four students during our writing block, and I work to do more listening to the writer than talking and teaching. Over the years, I've worked to ask more open-ended questions in writing conferences so that students do more thinking and talking, because I know that the person doing most of the talking is the person doing the learning. So, instead of my voice, I work to listen closely to writers' needs and intentions. These kinds of conversations nudge student agency and independence forward and give the young writer opportunities to wrestle with ideas and make decisions while I ask questions to ignite their own thinking and creativity. In a conference, you might hear me make statements like "Tell me more about your decision to . . ." or "Say more about what

Ben signs up for a conference.

> Much of what I do as a teacher of writing is to trust that learning isn't instantaneous but a process over time.

you're doing in this draft . . ." or ask questions like "Will you talk to me about the details of this illustration?" or "What would you like to share with me about your writing process today?"

Of course, it's normal to get a lot of "I don't know"s or shoulder shrugs at the beginning of the year, so the conversations that grow out of these questions certainly develop over time. Lots of times I hear myself asking, "But if you *did* know, what would you say?" At the beginning of the year, and more times than not, the children are able to talk about and name their process, struggles, and successes when I position myself with an expectant view of the learner. When I expect the writer to be able to talk about their work, they do, and we just trust that with daily interactions, that dialogue and those reflective processes will develop over time. Much of what I do as a teacher of writing is to trust that learning isn't instantaneous but a process over time.

Because this is a daily routine built into the workshop time, the writers expect this work to happen and know that students who confer with me will be the first writers to share during share time. Why? Because share time is an opportunity to get that one-on-one teaching out into the room and also to teach writers how to share their process and their learning with classmates. (More on writing share in the next section.)

At the back of each student's writer's notebook, we've made a section for notes, next steps, and "teaching points/writing reminders." Writers use these notes in their own work after our conferences, and they also share their teaching points or writing reminders with the class during writing share time. In the picture at the top of the next page, the three notes you see in Carter's notebook stemmed from the work he was doing in these three times I had a one-one-one conferences with him in September. In the first conference, we were thinking together about all the ways and all the places writers can get ideas. In the next conference, we focused on how mentor texts he's reading can sometimes support his writing work. The last conference was during our beginning-of-year poetry study, and we were learning about figurative language and ways poets communicate feeling and emotion with sound effects. These notes are quick reminders, and each teaching point may be an overarching writing goal, a tip, a specific technique, or a general writing practice—all dedicated to supporting the individual writer in those conferring moments.

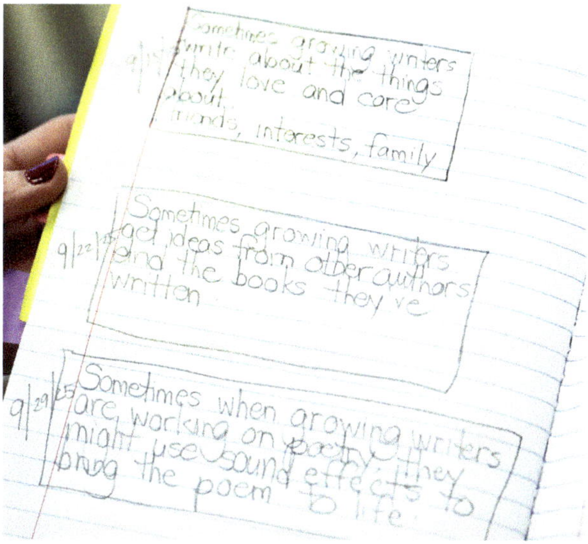

Carter's notes from three one-on-one conferences

Writing Share

Writing share time is a daily routine that quickly becomes a favorite across all classes and grade levels. One thing is true about most elementary writers who have a predictable writing time every day: They become confident as writers and are eager to share their work with others, so a time for sharing their work becomes critical to the growth, development, and engagement of every group of writers.

The writing share time routine is one way to encourage and honor that sense of agency in our students and center their voices so that creativity and imagination are on full display. I've been deliberate in thinking about ways to support students by shifting the focus of the writing share time from simply letting students read their in-process or published work to:

- Being intentional about supporting students in the language they use for both sharing and reflecting/commenting on a piece of writing
- Developing routines that help students see classmates' work as potential mentor texts
- Prepping writers for the multiple teaching opportunities during their share time
- Supporting writers in studying how writers imagine, create, craft, revise, edit, and share their work for an audience of readers

In our class this year, students needed support in how to lead a productive writing share without me at the center. One of the biggest goals I have for students is for them to feel confident in their abilities to lead and teach the class without me always interjecting my ideas and my voice over their every move. Of course, this kind of sharing takes scaffolding, and my voice is more dominant in the beginning-of-year writing share times when students aren't as sure of themselves or don't yet feel comfortable in carrying on a conversation or teaching a strategy to their peers without direct teacher support.

I learned long ago that when students see their names in print and recognize that their ideas and voices are valued, they become eager and willing to share their thoughts with classmates and their teachers.

This daily practice is critical so that, over time, students can and will take ownership and lead the learning; multiple goals are met at the same time. Students are not only learning about writing craft, structure, techniques, and ways to present their ideas to an audience, they're also learning how to become autonomous, agentive people who have the power and freedom to share their ideas and ask for honest feedback from others.

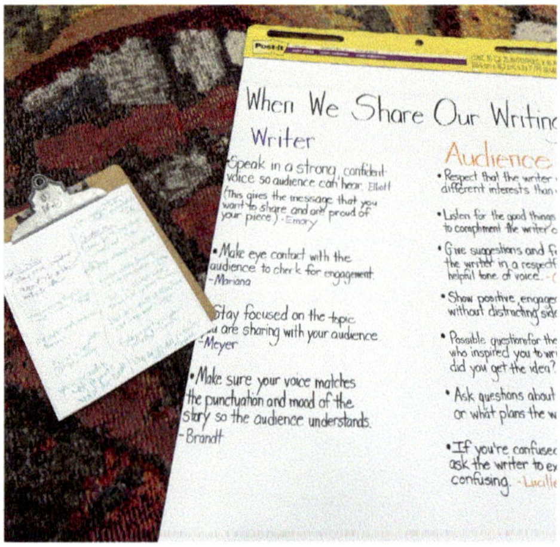

Two charts we've created early in the year (see top of next page) help scaffold the writers as they begin to share their work with partners or the whole class. All charts are co-created with the students sharing the ideas that are most helpful and worthy of making it to the charts. These charts then hang for as long as the students use and refer back to them throughout the year. When creating a chart, I first take notes on a clipboard, noting which student says what and then later transferring our collaborative thinking to the chart. (I'm unable to chart student thinking in neat and orderly ways in real time, and I don't want to waste a moment.) This is why I take notes first and then wait until there's quiet time for me to transfer the student thinking to the chart.

Sometimes, I quote students directly so that we can refer to the exact wording for help when going back to the charts in class. Other times, I summarize what students say, but I always record the students' names next to their ideas or quotes. I learned long ago that when students see their names in print and recognize that their ideas and voices are valued, they become eager and willing to share their thoughts with classmates and their teachers.

However, I do recognize that speaking in front of the class or even being ea-

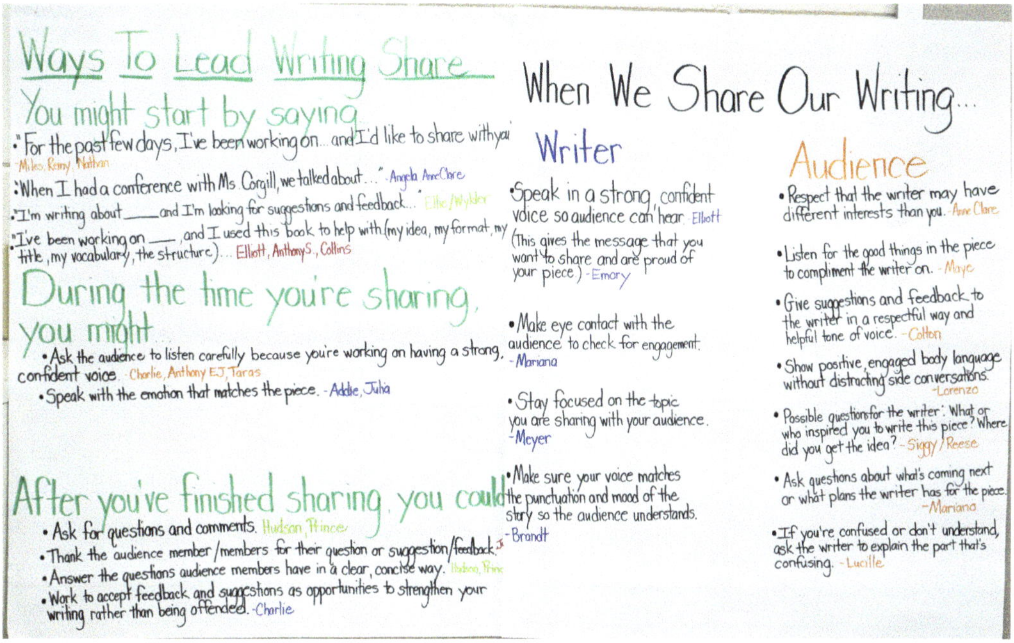

Writing share charts

ger to share work isn't easy or even desirable to some writers at first. One way I've found to support those students who may not feel comfortable sharing for a variety of reasons is to ask if they'd be willing for a classmate to partner with them to celebrate their work. Children are much more comfortable sharing with a trusted peer before sharing with an adult or entire classroom audience. More often than not, writers want others to hear their writing or see their illustrations or hear their storytelling, but speaking to an audience to share can be daunting. Having a classmate who is eager and willing to do the talking for them at first takes the pressure off and ensures that all voices are celebrated—even the quiet voices who aren't yet ready to speak up and speak out.

During share time, students take the lead and may do the following:

- Summarize their writing conference with me for the class to give the "why" behind their work for the day
- Share a text that inspired that writing work
- Read aloud their draft or in-process piece of writing
- Talk about decisions they made to add to or improve the draft
- Respond to feedback and compliments from classmates
- Answer questions from classmates about idea generation, craft moves, revision decisions, audience for the piece, or publication ideas

Anne Clare and Elliott share *Big Talk* by Paul Fleischman, the inspiration for their two-voice poem.

Anne Clare and Elliot

Both Anne Clare and Elliott wanted to work together in the beginning-of-year poetry study—friends who like to hang out but also like to write together. Why not let students write together if it sparks excitement and stamina to stick to a writing project? I initially shared several books written as "two-voice" poems with them to show what's possible if they did, in fact, choose to write a poem together.

Taras and Charlie share their two-voice poem with the class.

The poem, "Voice" by Charles Waters and Irene Latham from their book *Dictionary for a Better World* (2020) became a favorite partner poem (written for two voices) in the first weeks of school. Readers pored over it and practiced reading it aloud in partnerships for days during our reading-for-writing time.

"We want to write a poem about being friends, Ms. Corgill." I immediately thought of an older picturebook, *Being Friends* (2002) by Karen Beaumont, and pulled that book from the shelf to share with Anne Clare and Elliott. This book had a see-saw pattern and could be something they might try as they described each other as friends. The draft that Anne Clare and Elliott wrote became a touchstone text for the entire class, and soon after they shared that draft, a whole host of two-voice poems emerged.

Taras and Charlie were inspired by Anne Clare and Elliott and would linger beside the girls and ask questions during writing time for several days. This is the way that ideas are generated in class—not just by me, but by pulling up close to friends and learning from the other writers in the classroom.

Anne Clare, Elliott, Charlie, Taras, and Ella talk about their two-voice poems.

Prince

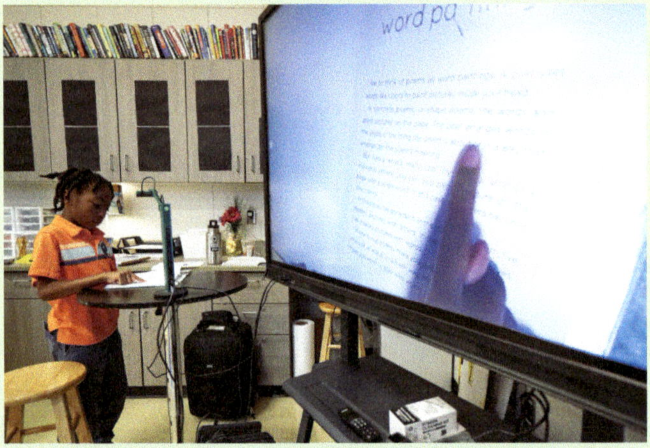

Prince points to a part in the text about word arrangement, explaining his decision to use this text as a mentor for his shape poem.

I noticed as I moved around the room to check in with the kids while they were reading poetry that Prince seemed drawn to the poetry books written or designed in the shape or pattern of the topic. He was fascinated with how poets were intentional about their word design on the page and how word placement helped strengthen meaning. Prince had noticed the cover of Nikki Grimes's poetry book *Words with Wings* (2013) and commented on how it looked like the words were flying off the page of the cover. He wanted to make his words fly, too. Prince also loves sports and is a Kwame Alexander fan and was reading *The Crossover* (2019) in independent reading. I reminded him how, in some parts of *The Crossover*, the author mimicked the movement of sports. He was interested in trying to write like these authors, and he wanted to explore other books with shape, pattern, and concrete ways to show meaning in his poetry. The book he's sharing in the picture above is another one he'd found that described to the class the technique he was trying in his writing. In writing share time, he got his classmates excited about trying to write some concrete poems of their own.

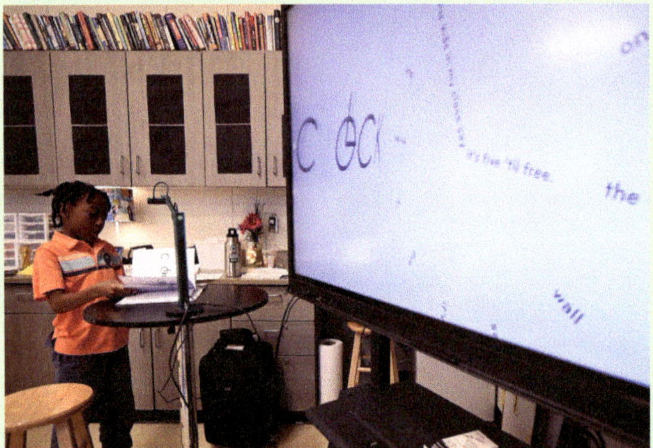

Prince shows the class the example of a poem written in the shape of the topic.

Daily Writing Share Chart Schedule

Time is always an issue in our teaching—not enough time to get it all done in the hours we're with the children. Every day, *LOTS* of students want to share their writing, and if everyone shared every day, that's all we'd do! Luckily, all "problems" in our class become teaching opportunities, and figuring out how to make sure we had an equitable, efficient writing share time was one of those "figure-outable" problems.

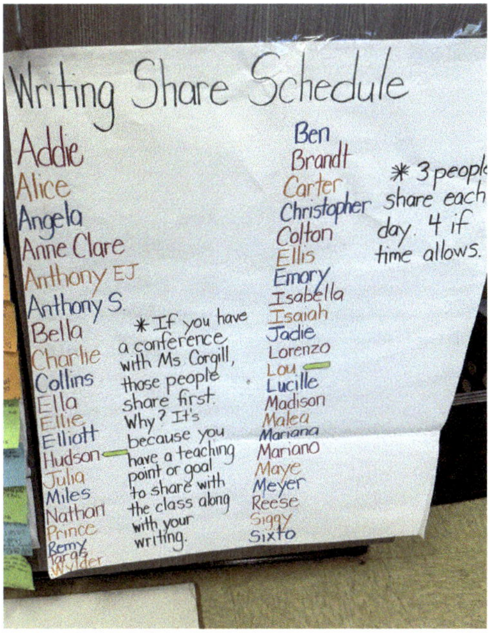

The writing share schedule helps structure this vital part of the writing workshop.

Since students know that they will be conferring with me often and that during those conferences, we set a goal or make a "teaching point" that needs to be shared with classmates, students decided that "people who confer with Ms. Corgill" should go at the top of the sharing schedule. If time allows, we then should follow a set schedule. The writing share chart showcases how students decided to make writing share happen every day and how we ensured there would be time to keep this ever-important part of the workshop in the daily routine.

Three to four people share every day. If Ms. Corgill has fewer than four conferences a day with the writers in our class, we automatically go to the alphabetized list to see who's next on the schedule to share. Problem solved!

Engagement becomes the norm when writers know that they are at the center of the decision making in the classroom. When students can feel and see their voices guiding our decisions and refining our routines, those routines become even more valuable and sustainable. I don't think up routines that make my life easier before the start of the year or even after school has started; student agency and centering student voices are my top priorities, so routines that foster agency and independence for children are also top priority. Daily routines create opportunities for children to develop agency and ownership in the work we do because they are predictable and have been co-created and firmly established by the children and me . . . together.

If You Want to Learn More about Building Writing Routines...

Cultivating Young Multilingual Writers: Nurturing Voices and Stories in and beyond the Classroom Walls, Tracey T. Flores and María E. Fránquiz (2023)

Tell Me More: Conferring with Artists, Writers, and Storytellers, Stella Villalba (2026)

How Do I Teach Talking and Listening to Build Writers' Identity and Independence?

We always hope that children will come to our rooms ready and confident to put their writing ideas on paper. However, I have learned over the years that writers believe that the ideas they put on paper have value when we also spend a lot of time speaking and listening to each other. In *Opening Minds: Using Language to Change Lives,* Peter Johnston reminds us that "our language choices have serious consequences for children's learning and for who they become as individuals and a community . . . the language we choose in our teaching changes the worlds children inhabit now and those they will build in the future" (p. 7).

Students must have opportunities to speak those ideas into existence and have practice talking about their thinking and ideas on a daily basis. The talk we practice today will create the spark for the talking, idea wrestling, and problem solving students will do tomorrow.

Partnerships That Ignite Conversations

The intentional practice of talking and listening is a key routine in our writer's workshop and in all parts of the day. It's easy to think that talking and listening are skills anyone just "knows how to do." However, there is much teaching that goes into teaching writers and readers how to talk and listen to one another, so the first months of school are filled with focus lessons centered on how to talk and listen and putting the supports in place to make sure these skills are honed and developed over the entire year.

What does that teaching around talking and listening look like? I start with a focus lesson on random partnerships the first week of school—pairing students to become talking partners whenever we gather as a whole group for a focus lesson, a read-aloud, a class share time, or a discussion. I draw popsicle sticks with student names on them from a cup for the partnership pairings to nudge students beyond their comfort zones. These random partnership pairings initiate an intentional time for students to get to know one another and become comfortable talking with students who aren't necessarily close friends (at least not yet!).

These partnerships stay the same for two weeks, and students sit next to their partner in a circle every time we gather together on the rug. The circular seating formation provides opportunities for us to build on those talking and listening skills while seeing each other face to face rather than sitting facing the backs of heads. We work on intentional, engaged body language—facing in the direction of the person speaking or making eye contact with the speaker while they are talking.

Ella and Nathan work together as talk partners.

Carter and Maye discuss a book as talk partners.

My Role

I typically sit in the circle with the students, sending the message that I am one of the group—shifting that balance of power so that children learn to see me just as one of the group of people who want to listen and build on the ideas of other students. My choice of seating also centers the students in the discussion so they don't default to me or look my way when speaking or answering a question.

Some phrases you might hear me say during our time together on the rug that nudge partners to practice speaking and listening to each other:

- **Who would like to share what your partner said?** This kind of question nudges children to practice active listening so that they can then report to the group what the partner said, and it also takes the focus off of sharing only what we want to share, elevating our classmates' voices first and foremost.
- **Who thinks differently?** This kind of question sends the message that we expect there to be a difference in opinions and ideas and that we build stronger understandings when there are a variety of voices, ideas, and opinions.
- **Who can add on to what ______ said?** This kind of question allows students time to make connections to the thinking of others while also building on an idea with additional information or opinions.
- **What did someone say today that you might try in your own writing?** This kind of question reminds students that there is always something that they can learn from each other, whether it's an idea to wrestle with or linger on or an idea or a strategy to try later in their own writing.
- **What questions do you have?** This kind of question sends the message that questions are encouraged and expected. It lets students know that I expect curiosity and wrestling with ideas. I prefer this approach to saying, "Does anyone have any questions?"
- **How might you solve that problem?** or **Who can answer this question for ______?** These kinds of questions shift the balance of power from teacher to student, sending the message to the writer(s) that I believe in their capabilities to find solutions to challenges they face instead of relying on me. Rather than focusing on the adult to jump in and fix the problems or provide all the answers, these questions put power and ownership into the hands of writers.

As we practice this talk together as a whole class, it becomes more natural for students to use what they've learned in writing partnerships and groups at all times of the day.

Using Books to Invite Conversations

One way to begin honoring writers' voices is my strategic selection of books we'll read aloud for each writing study throughout the year. I choose mentor texts that will elicit conversation and noticings or questions around a writing structure, crafting technique, or genre-specific characteristic. Each day, students have time at the beginning of the day (or at the beginning of their class period—I teach two classes of readers and writers this year, so their "reading-for-writing" time typically happens before the writing workshop begins). We start the class time with reading and sharing discoveries from the picturebooks. At the beginning of each writing study, we start a chart titled "What We're Discovering about ______" (poetry, in this case) at the beginning of the year.

Before a unit of study, I spend time carefully reading and selecting the books that will be the ones we study for discoveries. I make sure that I know what's inside each book and which genre-specific elements I want to highlight and teach the children to try in their writing. Knowing each book well is important so that I can direct students to particular pages in the text with elements of the genre I hope that they'll notice. For example, in Irene Latham's book *Fresh Delicious* (2016), there were lots of examples of similes and metaphors, so that book might be one I'd select to place on the shelf when we're studying figurative language in poetry.

Knowing the books is important, but ensuring that students have time to read and then talk about what they discover is

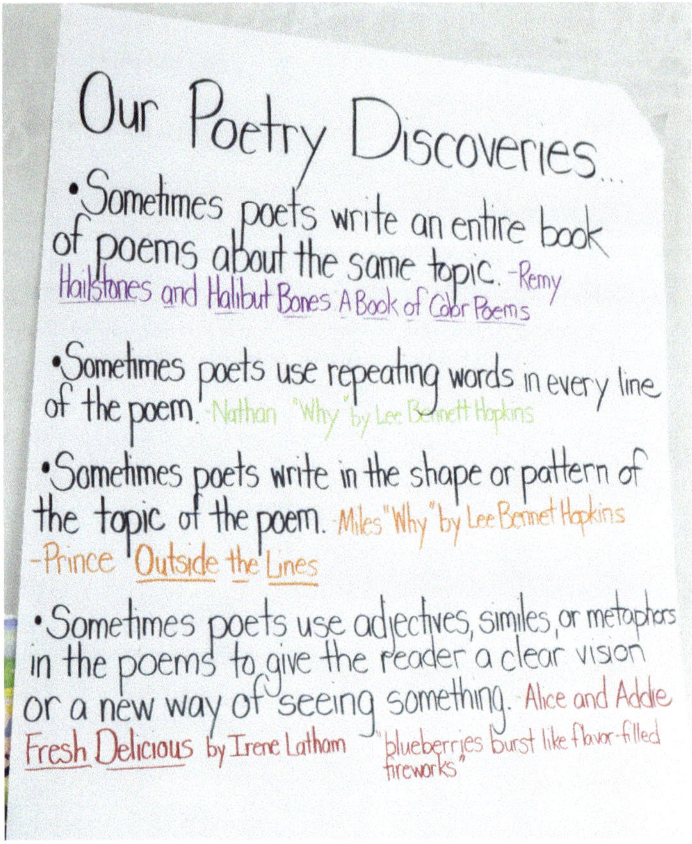

Our Poetry Discoveries chart

most critical during this time of the workshop. As students read and talk daily about their discoveries, they then begin to try out writing techniques, formats, and ways to use language in their own writing. They share ideas with classmates. Books that line the shelves of our classroom become the fuel for more writing discoveries and attempts to emulate these mentors we read and study each day. This doesn't happen quickly. It happens because this work becomes a predictable, daily routine, and students learn to count on this reading time as a place to study writers, their techniques, and to then try out the new learning as writers themselves.

Below, you'll find some questions and statements you might hear in our daily reading-for-writing time. Each of these offers space for students to think and talk together as partners or as a whole group about what they're learning and discovering about writing. At the beginning of the year, these conversations begin with simple answers because it takes practice for students to learn how to talk about what they notice as writers. Over time, the observations and ways students articulate their writing discoveries grow and evolve. The more we study a variety of authors, types of texts, different structures and crafting techniques, and spend time sharing those discoveries, the more sophisticated the students' writing discoveries become.

Prompts to Encourage Thinking and Conversation during Reading-for-Writing Time

- What might we add to our genre (poetry, nonfiction, fiction, etc.) discoveries chart today? Who would like to share?
- Turn to your partner and tell them one thing you learned from reading today that you might try in your own writing.
- Who has something they discovered in their poetry reading today? (Insert any genre in place of poetry depending on what you're studying with your students.)
- What books gave you new ideas for your writing today?
- How does the author of the book you read use ______, and how might you try that in your writing today? (This could be a format, a structure, a topic, a way to use language or new vocabulary, a genre-specific element, etc.)
- Who has tried ______? (This is referring to a specific discovery or statement on the co-created chart.) Would you mind sharing how you tried that in writing share today?
- Are there any books you'd like to add to our collection that might be helpful for classmates to read and get ideas?

Making Student Thinking Visible

As with our Poetry Discoveries chart, the way I capture student voices to honor their ideas and get them talking more is to take notes on everything they say and also have them write their own thinking on sticky notes—and then transfer that student thinking to anchor charts in the room. These co-created anchor charts become kindling for more conversation and a renewed willingness for those quiet voices (or not-so-quiet ones) to see that their words and ideas are important enough to document and highlight. I always write the students' names by their thinking, ensuring that everyone knows who made the statement. It somehow ignites more student sharing when others see that names go by each statement, which also gives us the opportunity, if needed, to dig deeper, asking the student to say more about that thought.

Student thinking that's captured and written on chart paper makes up the only anchor charts in the room for easy access and reference when needed. Over the years, I've learned that writers refer to the co-created charts far more often than ones

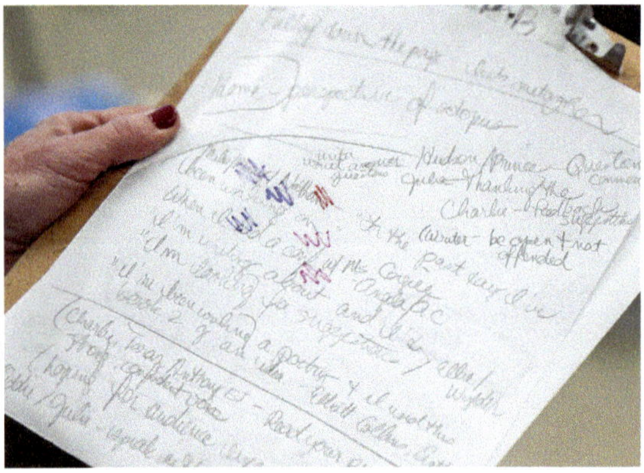

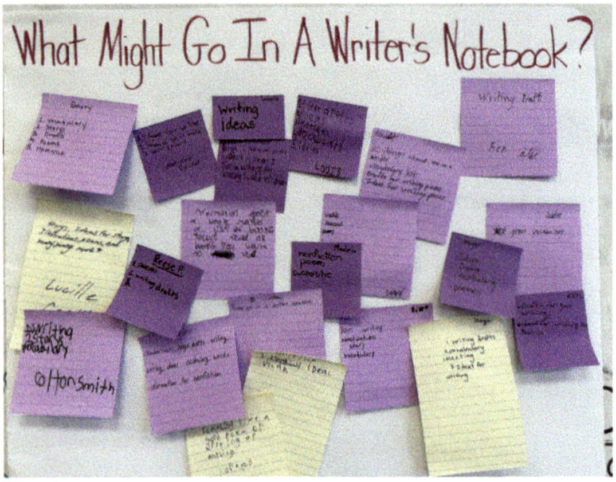

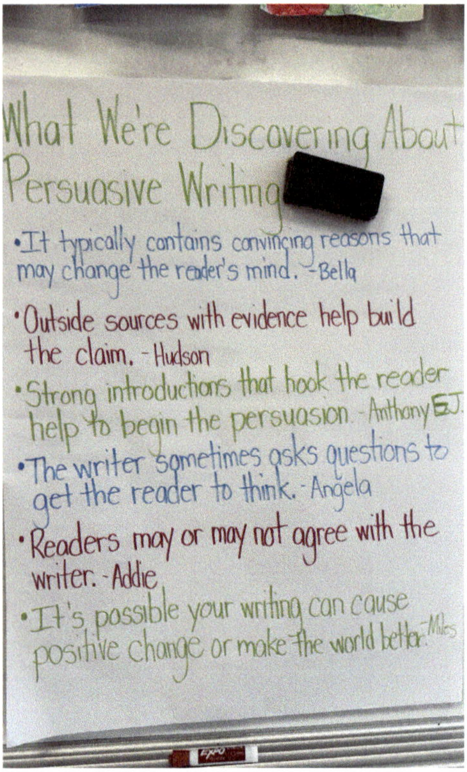

I make sure students' names accompany their thinking in my own notes and on anchor charts for the class.

that are premade or made only by me before a lesson or conversation, so I no longer make charts without student collaboration. It's the co-construction of knowledge that forms the foundation of all the learning in our classroom. It's the learning that sticks.

(No, you probably can't read my notes, but neatness and organization isn't the point here—it's getting student thoughts down in a way that I will later transfer to charts in the room. Capturing student thinking is what's most important, along with making sure I can read my own notes when it's time to create the chart!)

The photo immediately above was taken after the first nine weeks of school when we celebrated the ALA Youth Media Award winners. We'd been studying nonfiction, and this particular part of the study centered on the award criteria for the Robert Sibert Medal for nonfiction. You can see each award criteria on the board, rewritten in kid-friendly language. Students worked in groups to rephrase the criteria so we could understand the language and rate award contenders in our classroom, and then I made chart strips of their newly written criteria.

Elevating Student Voices in Writing Share

The chart at the bottom of this page was co-created during the first weeks of school as we learned about what would happen each day in writing share time. So often this part of writing time is left out in classrooms because "there's just not enough time." However, in my opinion, it's one of the most important times of the writing block, and it's where most of my direct instruction happens.

Writing share happens each day at the end of the writing block. When I'm thinking about timing for a writing block each day, we typically spend from 45 minutes to an hour in writing. At the beginning of the year, it's closer to 45 minutes until the writers build stamina and need extra time for their individual or partner work. The focus lesson lasts between five and 10 minutes (and I don't conduct a focus lesson every day). However, we write and share every single day, so independent writing lasts around 35–40 minutes and writing share runs 10–15 minutes (sometimes longer if engagement is high and lots of students are eager to share and teach the class what they're working on and what they're learning about as writers).

Writing share isn't just a time for students to read what they're working on in class; this time serves multiple instructional purposes. Yes, first and foremost, it is a regular opportunity for students to share what they're proud of as writers and to read aloud the pieces they're working on.

But it's also a time to intentionally support the rest of the class as they hone their listening skills and learn to ask questions

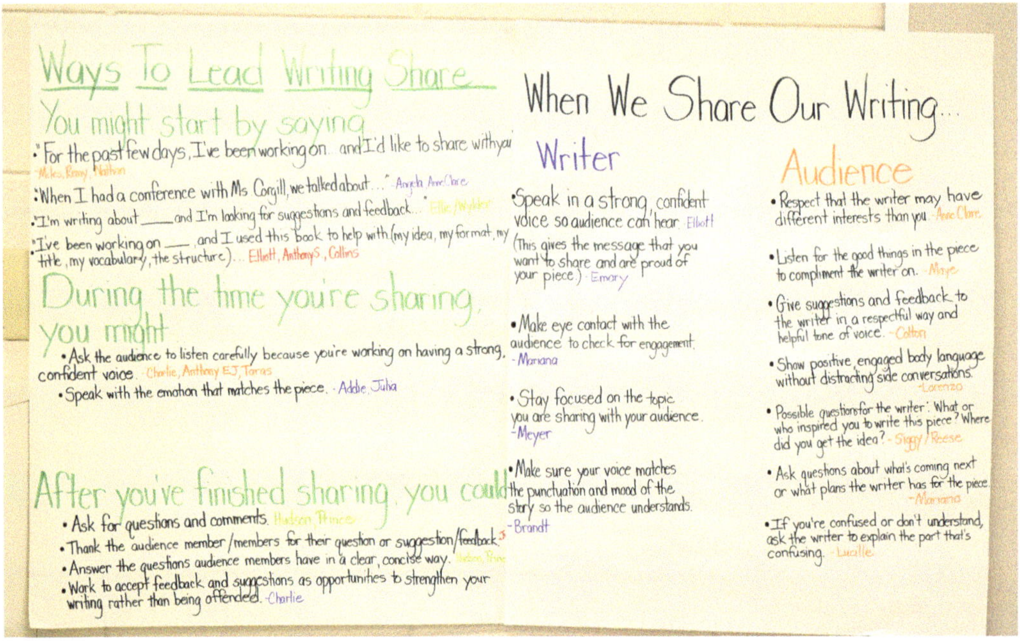

Taras shares Eloise Greenfield's *Thinker: My Puppy Poet and Me* (2019) to explain how this mentor text sparked an idea for his writing.

to lift the level of the writing that's being shared. And it's a time to teach young writers and listeners how to give and accept meaningful, specific feedback while also learning to compliment and name the good work already happening in the piece.

In the first few weeks of school, we think through possibilities of what might happen in all parts of the writing share and co-create anchor charts that writers can refer back to often until the writing share routine becomes second nature. This chart was co-created with my classes over several days at the beginning of writing share time—as we shared, students would reflect on ways we could improve the sharing time and do more than just read our pieces aloud. I always initiate the co-creation of a chart with a statement/question like this: "I'm noticing that we might be able to improve writing share so that more learning happens during this time every day. Can you turn and talk to your partner and think about some ways we might start the writing share? What might happen when someone is finished sharing their piece? How might we end the share time each day? Each of these may be a question I present over the course of a few days in order to give students time to think, process, share their ideas, and provide time for me to take notes so we can begin to build the anchor chart together.

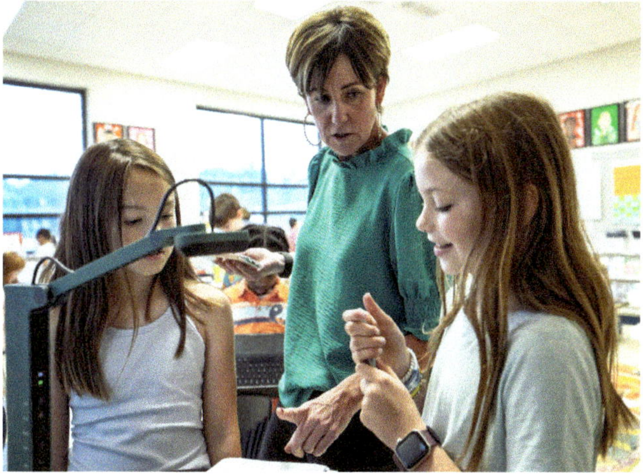

At the document camera, Julia and Alice rehearse and chat through what they'll teach the class when they share.

My Placement in the Room to Facilitate Writers' Speaking and Listening

When I first mentioned supporting talk in the classroom, I shared that I typically sit on the floor to shift the power dynamic, helping students see that my voice isn't the only one in the room and certainly shouldn't be the most powerful one. To strengthen student speaking and listening (especially to one another), I am also strategic about my positionality at all times of the day. Sometimes I sit in the rocking chair (usually for a read-aloud or to begin a conversation with one big question). Many times, I sit alongside students on the rug in the circle during our class discussions or share times. This signals to students that I'm just one voice in the room, and it ensures that students have practice speaking and looking at all classmates, not just turning to look at me when they answer. It levels the playing field and balances the power—I'm not the only teacher in the room, and I expect learners to trust that my voice isn't the only voice that's valued.

Once routines have been established and the writers are confident in those routines, I will sit at the back of the room or at the back of the circle when students

Sometimes I sit in the rocking chair to showcase a book or teach a lesson.

The kids listen to Siggy talk about her piece during writing share as I sit in the back of the classroom.

are facing away from me and listening to what classmates share. I may gently nudge with a question or a comment, but this is an opportunity for students to take the lead in the sharing and the discussion. I also move around the room during conferring, pulling up alongside writers to listen, support, question, and encourage them through their writing process. I ensure that my voice isn't front and center in all teaching or conversations, and my strategic placement in the room during lessons, conferring, and sharing time supports that work to lift student voices.

I point out a particular part to highlight on the anchor chart as the writers begin to share.

If You Want to Learn More about Teaching Speaking and Listening...

Building Bigger Ideas: A Process for Teaching Purposeful Talk, Maria Nichols (2019)

Choice Words: How Our Language Affects Children's Learning, Second Edition, Peter H. Johnston (2024)

Hands Down, Speak Out: Listening and Talking across Literacy and Math, Kassia Omohundro Wedekind and Christy Hermann Thompson (2020)

Opening Minds: Using Language to Change Lives, Peter H. Johnston (2012)

How Do I Identify and Use Mentor Texts to Support Writers?

Writers may come to your classroom having few experiences with creating their own pieces of writing or imagining the possibilities for what could be. It's important to build a core collection of texts that can do just that—help learners imagine the possibilities and ignite new ideas or ways for communicating through writing, illustrating, and storytelling.

We want books at our fingertips that support a child's vision, speak to their interests, offer views of the world that both mirror their identities or open their eyes to the world beyond their own lived experiences. As we learned from Dr. Rudine Sims Bishop in her 1990 "Windows, Mirrors, and Sliding Glass Doors" essay, "When there are enough books available that can act as both mirrors and windows for all our children, they will see that we can celebrate both our differences and our similarities, because together they are what make us all human."

We must read widely and know books, but we must also create intentional spaces filled with the texts that can fully support and mentor every child. When I think about identifying mentor texts for writers, I think in two categories: picturebooks and digital media.

Picturebooks and Digital Media as Mentor Texts

When I'm selecting picturebooks or digital media that will support writers in my classroom, these are the questions and big ideas I start with when selecting texts that help me make wise decisions when purchasing texts or offering digital media support to the learners in my classroom.

In Kristin Ziemke's book *Text and Tech: Reading All Ways in K–8* (2025), she reminds us to take the "yes, and" stance in choosing mentor texts for our writers and readers. "We say yes to print and celebrate all it offers our students while also saying 'and' to digital because we acknowledge that these texts can build upon what we do with books and offer new ideas, accessibility, and opportunities. Lifelong literacy is not a binary either/or scenario" (p. 16).

Questions When Considering a Work as a Mentor Text:

- What specific part of this book or digital text/tool shows a clear example of a structure, a crafting technique, a unique use of language, or an illustration technique that a writer could try?
- Is this text one in which the writers represented in this room see themselves? Can they identify with this book and advance their learning of their own identity or that of others?
- Is this text written by an own-voices author—a writer or illustrator who brings their lived experience and expertise to the text so readers can see themselves and others accurately reflected in the text?
- Is this book one that could be part of a collection or a text set that further supports a writer with a common structure, technique, or idea that's found in other, similar books?
- Is this book designed for elementary readers to independently read, navigate, and understand?
- Is this a book children at my students' grade level might be intrigued by based on the title and cover illustrations?
- Is it one that brings memories to life and naturally causes children to make connections to their own lives and experiences?
- Is this a book that has a clear structure or pattern that young writers could identify and emulate?
- Is the language in this book rich and varied to not only help strengthen and widen the writer's/reader's vocabulary but also to embed and use in their own writing?
- Can I see myself using this book for a whole-class or small-group focus lesson to teach a crafting technique, share a topic idea, invite writers to explore the language in the text, or study the illustrator's style or technique?
- Is this a book that could become a partner, support, or "friend" for a writer?
- Does this book fit our age or grade developmental level? Is it something kids at this age would be curious about or find interesting?

Following is a short list of just a few texts or websites I might use as mentors for writers at the very beginning of the year. This list is certainly not a comprehensive list or collection; it's designed to give you an idea of the kinds of books I might choose to share with writers early in the year (more specifically, texts that match the questions I might ask myself when choosing books). These books are designed to give writers a vision of what's possible in their own writing, with text, illustrations, and ideas that are simple and relatable to encourage and not overwhelm the writer.

Alma and How She Got Her Name by Juana Martinez-Neal (2018)

This is a beautiful story of a young girl who thinks, "My name is too long, Daddy." Writers learn from reading this story that each part is a tribute, honoring the relative who is part of this child's name and history. Alma Sofia Esperanza José Pura Candela comes to realize that her name fits her perfectly, and this book is a fantastic mentor for writing around our names and the beauty and story behind them.

Big Sister, Little Sister by LeUyen Pham (2023)

This story explores the relationship between a younger and an older sibling, one with which many children can identify. Also, students without siblings can make connections with their own friendships and relationships across age ranges. The text is accessible for elementary readers and writers, with simple sentence structures and a back and forth writing pattern. It's one that gives writers a vision for what's possible in writing about sibling relationships or friendships. It's also a great model for older students who are studying how to write for and engage younger audiences.

The Colors of Us by Karen Katz (2002)

This book is helpful as we're working to create our self-portraits and celebrating the differences and beauty we bring to the classroom. Writers begin many years writing lots about their own histories and identities, and this book captures ways to do that. It's also a nice mentor for our beginning poetry work, when we're learning to describe and compare items and people and ideas in rich and surprising ways: "My name is Lena, and I am seven. I am the color of cinnamon. Mom says she could eat me up." "Isabella is cupcake brown, like the cupcakes we had for her birthday."

Like Lava in My Veins by Derrick Barnes, illustrated by Shawn Martinbrough with Adriano Lucas (2023)

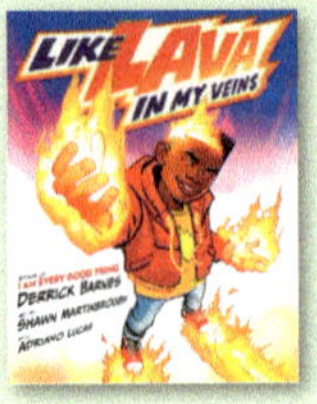

This title immediately grabs the attention of writers and readers alike with its superpower-themed graphic novel layout. Talk bubbles and text boxes support the comic book style that gives writers a vision of "I can do this kind of writing!" Underneath is a story of universal experiences like managing emotions and learning about empathy.

Friends Beyond Measure: A Story Told with Infographics by Lalena Fisher (2023)

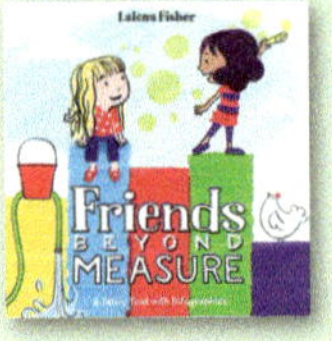

This is a lovely mentor for helping writers see the variety of ways they can communicate a message to a reader—not just through words but through infographics. It's a story of friendship, and it gives writers unique ideas about how to represent and describe their friendships with one another. The back matter is notably helpful, showing writers all the ways the author communicated her message of friendship through different infographics—from Venn diagrams to timelines to calendars and flow charts. This is an ideal book for math teachers as well!

Big by Vashti Harrison (2023)

Big gives writers a vision for ways to use two-page spreads and illustrate or write across pages with intentional use of color and font sizes to show emotion and create meaning. It's a text that has influenced writers but also speaks deeply to students navigating body image and self-love. It's a touchstone text for us on how to push back against harmful words and act in powerful ways to heal ourselves and others.

One Day, The End: Short, Very Short, Shorter-Than-Ever Stories by Rebecca Kai Dotlich, illustrated by Fred Koehler (2015)

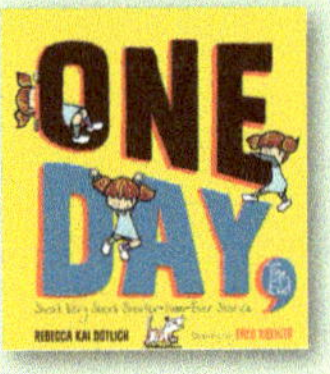

Using works with minimalist writing and stories that are intentionally incomplete, writers are eager to fill in the gaps and tell the rest of the story. This is a perfect mentor for elementary students because it makes writing feel more accessible to students and gives them the feeling that "I can do that!" This book also teaches children that their illustrations add to the details and offer subplots to the story. This book always ignites conversation, laughter, and new ideas and drafts for writers in the classroom.

Isabel and Her Colores Go to School by Alexandra Alessandri, illustrated by Courtney Dawson (2021)

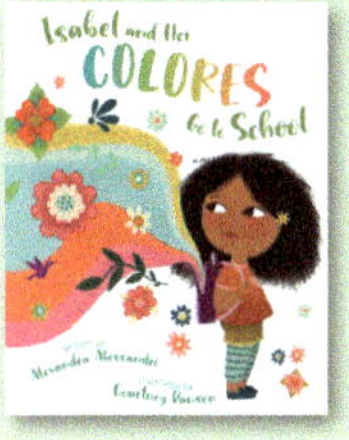

A mentor for writers, this text shows how the main character uses colors and drawings to overcome language barriers at school. This book reminds writers that their lived experiences and home languages are welcomed and are important parts of how they communicate and share their identities with others. The text offers translanguaging ideas for writers, with a dual language glossary and ideas for multilingual learners creating their own stories and books.

Maybe Something Beautiful: How Art Transformed a Neighborhood by F. Isabel Campoy and Theresa Howell, illustrated by Rafael López (2016)

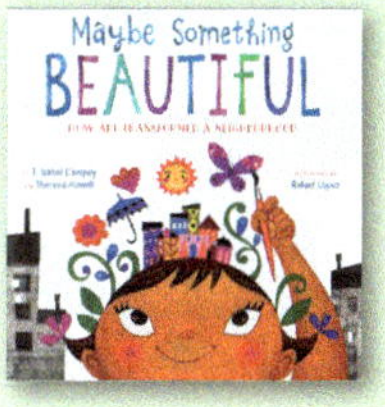

Calling all elementary-aged doodlers, illustrators, and mural lovers! Here's a book for you. This book is a powerful mentor text for those children in your classroom who tell their stories through art, those who are drawn to the marker box, tempera sticks, and watercolor collections. The book is based on a true story of the Urban Art Trail in San Diego, California, and shows young illustrators how storytelling through mural art can transform lives.

Super Goat Girl by Tracey Baptiste, illustrated by Dapo Adeola (2025)

This highly engaging text uses a recess scene to show the superpowers of contrasting characters (one that's familiar and relatable to elementary children). With the text written in comic book style, the book helps writers imagine how they might tell contrasting stories of characters in panels, talk bubbles, and text boxes, with bold, vivid colors.

Animal Poems of the Iguazú by Francisco X. Alarcón, illustrated by Maya Christina Gonzalez (2014)

This book is a great mentor text for multiple studies. For poetry, it's a perfect example of how a multilingual writer might try writing poems in two languages. Elementary writers love writing about animals, and this text offers opportunities for us to study and research interesting animals in the rainforest. It also shows writers how to teach other readers about those animals in a genre or format other than expository writing—beautiful poems that are sometimes shaped like the animal they describe, along with mixed-media artwork give writers and illustrators new ideas and visions for their own pieces.

How Do I Help Children Begin to Read Like Writers?

> *They [students] need to choose mentors who can teach them about detail and character development. They need to stand in front of the classroom and have time to share their images of good writing. They need to meet the challenge of finding just the right words to convey what they love about their favorite writers.*
>
> —SHELLEY HARWAYNE,
> *Lasting Impressions: Weaving Literature into the Writing Workshop* (1992, p. 156)

Read-Aloud

We must read to children every day. Not once in a while. **Every. Single. Day.**

What a grand opportunity to celebrate and study the work of beloved authors who can teach children through the beauty of their words and illustrations! Read-aloud has different purposes in my instruction, but this is one of the very first ways I begin to help children see themselves as authors of the kinds of texts we read aloud.

Reading aloud to children gives time for me to highlight beautiful language, interesting text features and structures, synergistic illustrations, rich vocabulary, and a multitude of ideas for how and what students might write about or try out in their own notebooks, drafts, and published pieces. As we read aloud together, we begin to gather books on the facing-out shelves (the shelves I spoke about in earlier sections) to give students a reminder and a place to go to read books that will help them study the techniques of the writer or illustrator.

Focus Lessons

The short, five- to 10-minute lessons at the beginning of a writing block are also great times to share mentor texts and point out specific craft / structure / language / illustration moves the writer or illustrator made. This is an intentional time to teach students to see that our reading lives inform our writing lives. We must look through the lens of the writer / illustrator when we're studying a text to get ideas for our own writing.

Mentor Text Matchmaking Conference

There are times when students are working on drafts or stuck and not sure how to proceed. This is another time I find mentor texts helpful for showing a writer what's possible and helping them see what a writer or illustrator is doing that is very similar to the work they're trying to do in their own pieces. This is also why it's important to know your students well and have a go-to set of mentor texts you know and can share quickly with a student. Knowing books from a writer's perspective takes time, but it's critical in the development of your writers. I suggest Katie Wood Ray and Stella Villalba's book, *Wondrous Words: Reimagining Writers and Writing in the Elementary Classroom* (2025), to give you an in-depth understanding of how we do this work of teaching children to read like writers and learning to read like writers ourselves.

A few beginning-of-the year guiding questions for helping students think about these books from a writer's or illustrator's perspective:

- Take a look at the words on each page of the text. What decisions did the author make about the placement of words on the page? Are they in text boxes? Bullets? Dialogue bubbles? Captions?
- Take a look at the illustrations on this particular page but don't read the words. What story is the illustrator telling on this page? How might you illustrate in the way this illustrator does?
- Listen as I read these few pages. What do you hear in the writing as I read? Is it a back and forth / see-saw pattern? Is one person talking? Is it a conversation between two or more characters?
- Read this page aloud (or listen to me read it). What interesting words or surprising vocabulary do you hear?
- Flip through each page in the book. How did the author organize the information across the pages of this book?
- Take a look at the cover/end pages/back matter/copyright and dedication pages. What do these pages do to teach the reader or help the reader understand and enjoy the book even more?

Any time I'm reading aloud to or alongside the children, these teachable reading moments can also become teachable writing moments, opportunities for me to ask, "Do you hear or see something you'd like to try in your own writing?" Intentional times with read-aloud, sharing a mentor text in a focus lesson, and matching books to writers are all necessary building blocks for helping give students a vision of what they might try or what they might create.

I sit in front of the class for a read-aloud.

I show part of the book on the document camera.

Depending on the type of text (or the class preference), I either read aloud from the rocking chair as students gather around or I share a text on the document camera for closer observations and conversation about a text.

Student Writing as Mentor Texts

Once students begin to see books as mentors for their own writing and are trying out techniques from a variety of texts in the room, new student work begins to emerge. Many times, student writing becomes the seed for growing new pieces of writing in the classroom. Once a student tries a technique, a format or structure, or uses ideas from books we've read, their work can (and should) be an example for other writers. In *Talking, Drawing, Writing: Lessons for Our Youngest Writers* (2007), Martha Horn and Mary Ellen Giacobbe speak about the significance of student work as mentors for classmates. "We believe more than ever that the writing of other children, including their own published pieces, are most powerful in providing them with a vision for how to approach their own writing" (p. 39). Daily share time gives students the opportunity to read and share their writing using the document camera, and this gives other writers ideas and inspiration for their own pieces.

I would recommend beginning to build a collection of student writing so that you can bring the ideas and published pieces of former and current writers to your classroom of current students. Using student writing as mentor texts lifts the level of the work of all writers, and because the work is written by same-age peers, it seems doable and possible and within a writer's reach in ways that published texts sometimes can't.

During our first unit of poetry, we had a series of friends writing "two-voice poems" on a variety of topics. Once a couple of students shared their "Being Friends" poem, new poems emerged from this one idea, from friendship to a lunch lady mom poem to potty humor bathroom poetry.

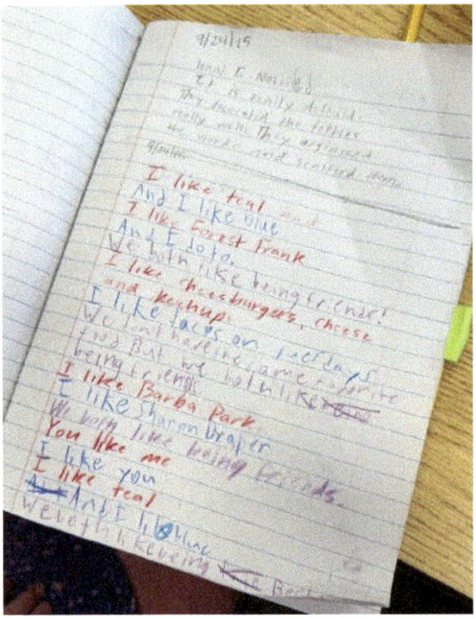

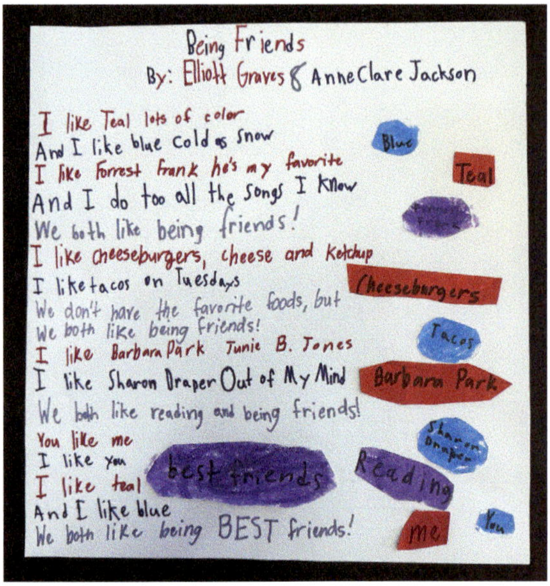

Anne Clare and Elliott's notebook draft of their two-voice poem and the final, published version of "Being Friends"

Remy and Bella share their two-voice poem about Remy's mom, who cooks our favorite lunches in the lunchroom.

The final, published version of "The Lunch Lady"

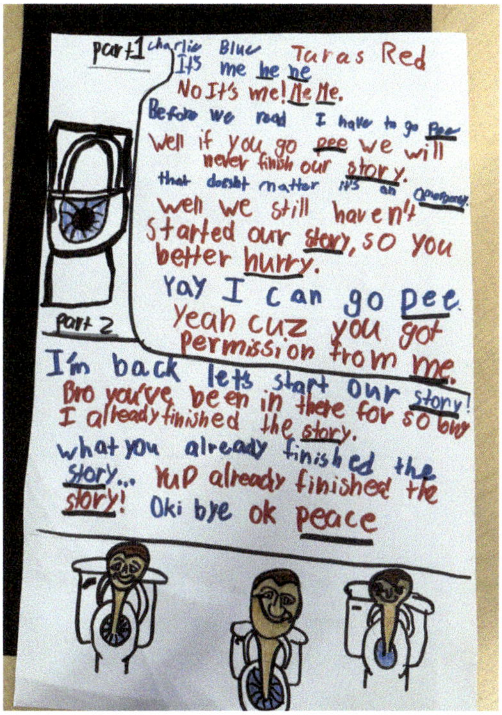

After publishing, Taras's and Charlie's poem made its way to the door of the boys' bathroom!

Sometimes, just one or two mentor texts will spark student publications that ignite writing for more classmates. Once a student read *Isabel and Her Colores Go to School* (2021) by Alexandra Alessandri and a few other students read *Hailstones and Halibut Bones: Adventures in Poetry and Color* by Mary O'Neill (1990), a group of students tried writing their own "orange" and "blue" poems. Soon after students shared these color poems, we had the full rainbow of color poems written and ready to be shared and displayed in the classroom, inspired by mentor texts.

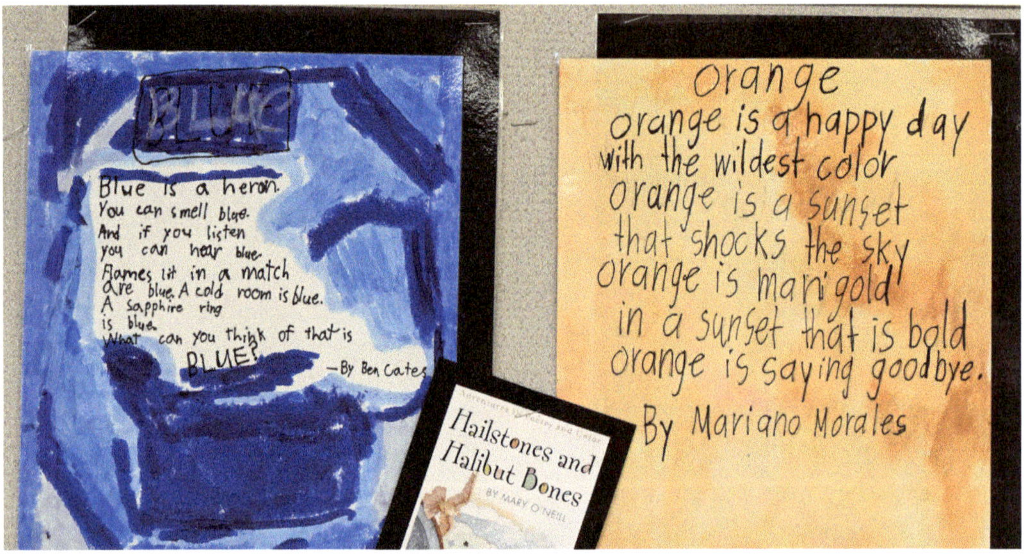

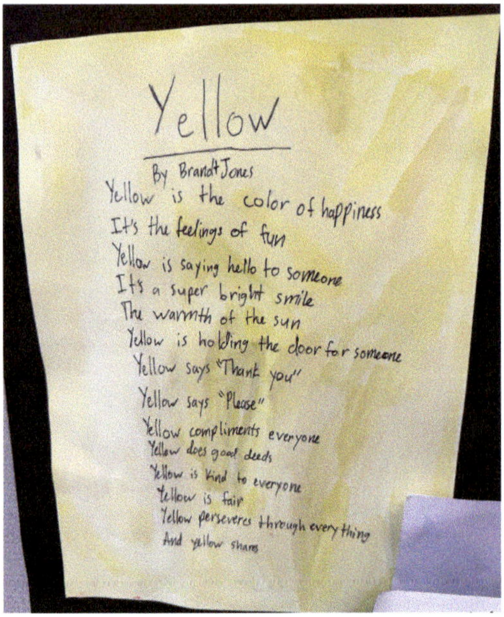

Several students wanted to try acrostic poems after a classmate shared, and soon we had groups of writers studying and writing acrostic poems.

What's important to note here is that when students begin the year sharing their writing in a daily, predictable fashion, they begin to learn from each other as mentors. Student writing is amplified and celebrated daily, and this ignites new writing and new ideas for other students in the room. It isn't necessarily the type of poem—acrostic poems or two-voice poems or color poems—that we are celebrating and amplifying. It's the idea that a student or group of students tried something as a writer because they saw a peer do it, and students begin to learn that books and fellow writers can become strong and powerful mentors for their own writing.

Once writers recognize that their classmates are authors to learn from, the possibilities for learning from mentor texts written by the authors lining the shelves and sitting in the seats of our classroom are limitless.

Resources for Curating a Collection of Mentor Texts

The way I curate a collection of books for students each year has evolved and will continue to change as I learn more about how to support and represent the diverse identities in my classroom.

I'm grateful to colleagues who continue to inform my thinking about how and why I choose particular texts for my classroom of writers and readers. I recognize that I have much to learn and continue to learn as I unpack, disrupt, and come face to face with the biases I hold. Becoming intentional about my own critical literacy has shaped how I live my life but also how I choose texts that will live as examples for children in my classroom.

> The kind of classroom library you build, develop, and maintain is at the heart of growing strong writers and readers.

I've learned that slowly building a rich, diverse, highly curated collection matters more than just making sure I have a lot of books in the room and on the shelves. So, if you're like me and want the best for your writers, give yourself time to build the strongest collection of mentor texts possible.

Curating a collection of books that show children what's possible is part of being a writing teacher. Writing and reading cannot be separated, so if you hope to develop strong writers, you must also be committed to developing lifelong readers. The kind of classroom library you build, develop, and maintain is at the heart of growing strong writers and readers.

On the opposite page are some people and sources I've learned from and return to often to get suggestions for new additions to my classroom library. Reading reviews and subscribing to quarterly journals, either online or in print, are great ways to keep up with what's current and which books are getting rave reviews.

Membership in professional organizations like NCTE also affords multiple opportunities to meet, engage with, and receive books from authors and publishers that you want your students to know and grow to love!

Online Resources for Building Book Knowledge

The Adventures of Library Girl! (Jennifer LaGarde)
www.librarygirl.net/

American Indians in Children's Literature
(Debbie Reese and Jean Mendoza)
americanindiansinchildrensliterature.blogspot.com/

American Library Association Youth Media Awards
www.ala.org

Disrupt Texts
(Tricia Ebarvia, Lorena German, Julia Torres, and Kim Parker)
disrupttexts.org/

Fuse 8 n' Kate **podcast**
available through most podcast providers

Horn Book Guide and quarterly journal
www.hbook.com/

Journal of Children's Literature
www.childrensliteratureassembly.org/journal.html

NCTE Children's Book and Poetry Awards
ncte.org/awards/ncte-childrens-book-awards/

If You Want to Learn More about How to Use Mentor Texts to Teach Writing and Build Your Classroom Library...

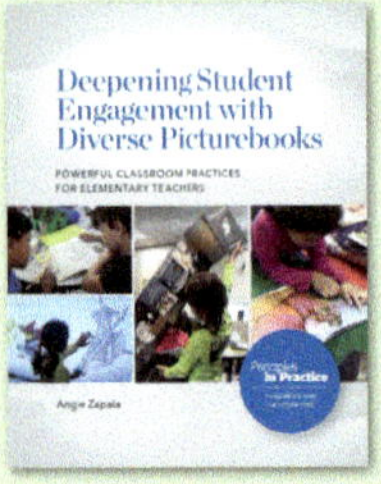

Deepening Student Engagement with Diverse Picturebooks: Powerful Classroom Practices for Elementary Teachers, Angie Zapata (2024)

Judging a Book by More Than Its Cover: A Critical Guide to Choosing Children's Literature, Laura M. Jiménez (2026)

Reading and Teaching with Diverse Nonfiction Children's Books: Representations and Possibilities, Thomas Crisp, Suzanne M. Knezek, and Roberta Price Gardner (eds.) (2021)

Wondrous Words: Reimagining Writers and Writing in the Elementary Classroom, Katie Wood Ray and Stella Villalba (2025)

How Do I Document Writers' Growth at the Beginning of the Year?

What Counts as Data?

Writers who grow write daily. If children have daily opportunities to put ideas to paper (or keyboard), linger over drafts, get feedback, and share their work, they grow in multiple ways.

Yet sometimes we miss the ways that good change shows up. If we don't take the time to pay attention to and document the smallest of writing developments, we miss out on meaningful data that can inform our instruction and help us (and our students) see the growth that's right in front of our eyes.

We must be intentional about looking for *all* the ways we see our writers developing and to count that as meaningful data—beyond the score on the standardized test or the letter grade on the report card. It's also a reminder that daily writing time in our classrooms is nonnegotiable if we want our students to make significant growth and improvement in their ability to generate, craft, and publish meaningful pieces of writing. The key to documenting all writing growth is to focus on strengths-based assessment and seeing students through an asset lens. These seemingly small ideas can be big reminders for how we can track and celebrate growth.

In the first nine weeks of school, the kind of teaching I do is really about what it's like to live like a writer and do the things that real writers do, day in and day out. With that in mind, the growth I'm looking for and documenting is centered mainly around writing identity, writing habits and understandings, and writers' attitudes and engagement rather than development of a particular writing skill or craft. Children must believe in their abilities as writers and be engaged in their daily work, first and foremost. In *What You Know by Heart: How to Develop Curriculum for Your Writing Workshop*, Katie Wood Ray says, "We have to get comfortable with the fact that students need help understanding how it is a person does this writing work, that they need these understandings just as much as they need to know where apostrophes go or different options for structuring a text or how to write compelling leads" (2002, p. 12).

Before I home in on teaching specific skills and techniques that writers use as they draft, revise, and publish their own pieces, we work together on our writerly stance. What does that mean? It's the development over time of a disposition, a sense of agency, the "I can do this" feeling that is critical if we want to teach children to become skillful, successful writers. I want to nurture and encourage and help writers see themselves through that asset lens as well, watering and tending to and growing the seeds of "I am a writer" in the hearts of children. Then, we can grow and develop specific writing skills, like conventional spelling, paragraphing, vocabulary development, deep understandings of genre characteristics, and application of those elements in drafts and published pieces.

Today's Date

Teaching your writers to date their papers seems so insignificant, but change over time is never clearer than when putting two pieces of writing side by side and looking at ways a writer grows from one date to the next. It's easy to categorize work and help young writers look for improvements and changes in their own work and to believe in the power of putting pencil to page day after day. It's fun to watch a writer sit alongside two pieces, one from August and one from May, and have a conversation about what's changed. So simple yet powerful!

Starting early in the year asking students to think about their writing growth sets students up to be able to reflect not just on attitude and engagement but to consider more specific writing knowledge and development as the year progresses (see example on next page).

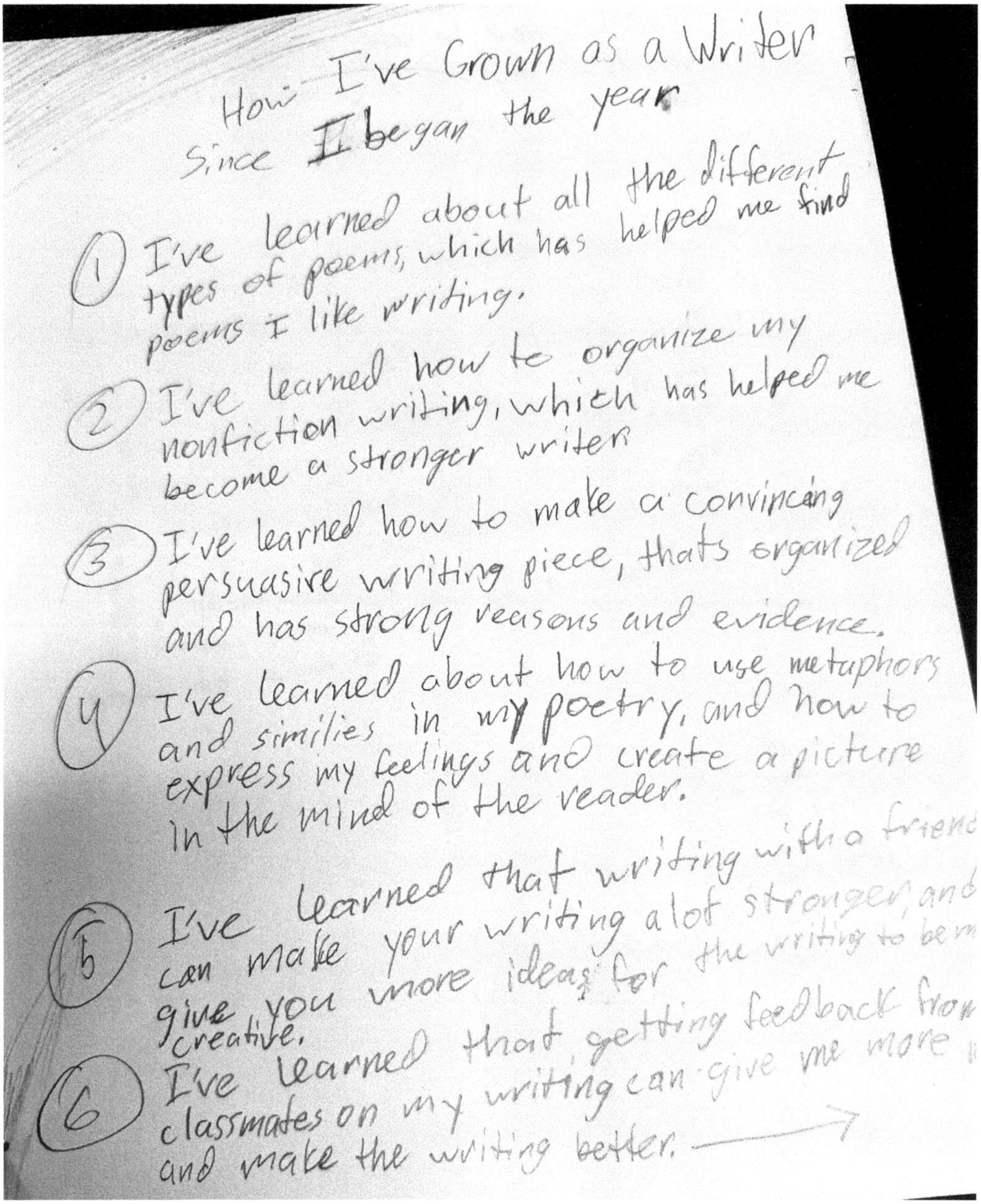

How I've Grown as a Writer
Since I began the year

1. I've learned about all the different types of poems, which has helped me find poems I like writing.
2. I've learned how to organize my nonfiction writing, which has helped me become a stronger writer
3. I've learned how to make a convincing persuasive writing piece, thats organized and has strong reasons and evidence.
4. I've learned about how to use metaphors and similies in my poetry, and how to express my feelings and create a picture in the mind of the reader.
5. I've learned that writing with a friend can make your writing a lot stronger, and give you more ideas for the writing to be m creative.
6. I've learned that getting feedback from classmates on my writing can give me more i and make the writing better. →

A student's reflection on their growth as a writer

Stamina and Time Spent Writing

Paying attention to changes in a group of writers' sustained writing work over blocks of time is another way to celebrate growth. Moving from just a few minutes of uninterrupted writing time at the beginning of the year (say 10–15 minutes) to longer blocks of work (like 30 minutes) to moments when students beg for "just 10 more minutes, please!" at the end of an hour-long block are signals for you as a teacher to know that writers are growing—growing in their stamina but also growing in their engagement for the writing work at hand. It's also a time for you to reflect back on the time writers are asking for and figure out ways to increase that time while chipping away at unnecessary time snatchers—like working with writers to shorten transitions or revise and tighten lessons that are unnecessary or go a bit longer than needed. Take the opportunity to reflect on these differences with your writers. Naming the positive change sets the tone for an even greater commitment from your writers when they see that you recognize their growth in the time they spend (and want to spend!) on writing.

100 Things about Me as a Writer

Several years ago, my friend Franki Sibberson shared an idea she tried with her readers called "100 Things about Me as a Reader." In a blog post, she talked about how this beginning-of-year work sets the stage for talk about reader identity for the whole year and sets students up to regularly reflect on their reading and growth, so I thought, "Why not try this for writing?" Even after many years of teaching, I'm still thinking about how to refine my practice and deepen student agency, independence, and habits that ignite and sustain learning across the year. This is one way to give writers the opportunity to see and document their understanding and development as a writer over time. Patterns emerge, and writers learn from each other as the year goes on. It's a powerful piece of documentation to share with families and administrators at the beginning, middle, and end of the school year.

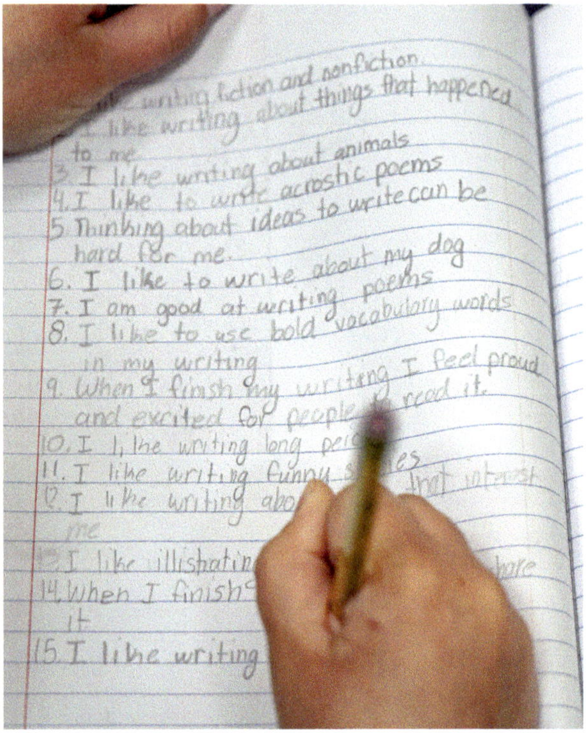

In-Process Celebrations

Sometimes it's more valuable to gather an audience for a celebration during the work, before pieces are published. Especially at the beginning of the year, an "in-process celebration" gives writers an opportunity to showcase the challenges, the idea development, the edits, the revisions, and the productive struggle that they face when working toward a final published piece. Inviting parents, colleagues, and administrators in during this part of the process is a powerful way to showcase the growth, development, and stamina of your writers.

Writing Journey Folders: Naming Growth in Ideas, Drafts, and Final Published Pieces with Photographs and Student Work

At the end of a writing study, collecting all parts of the work throughout the process instead of simply celebrating the final piece is one way to honor growth. We collect all evidence of work toward a published piece and house it in a two-pocket folder labeled "My Writing Journey." If necessary, you can easily develop scoring rubrics for each part of the process and have students reflect on their changes using the rubrics.

Writers at work

Angela is prepping for her Writing Journey folder collection at the end of the first nine weeks.

Published pieces are gathered for our first Writing Journey celebration.

Writing Attitude and Engagement Self-Reflections

In Carla Shalaby's book, *Troublemakers: Lessons in Freedom from Young Children at School,* we're reminded that "classrooms are places where children must be treated with reverence and dignity as free persons; spaces for children to lift up their voices—individually and collectively, in harmony and cacophony—and say what they really need and who they are" (2017, p. xii). Another way to lift our students' voices and showcase growth and development with your writers might be a short written or oral reflection about the changes your students see in themselves as writers and readers and people who have important ideas.

Throughout the year, I ask my readers and writers to complete a self-reflection on their growth. Many times, the reflection questions center on ideas about how their reading and writing attitudes, abilities, and ideas have changed over the course of the year. However, this first reflection goes back to my teaching about living a writerly life and centers mostly on the writer's attitudes and engagement, as you can see in the student responses on the following pages.

A child's thinking around what's working and what's challenging helps to focus my attention on specific needs and wants across our writing block. Reflection is an opportunity to honor their lived experiences and take what students tell us to build and refine our future lessons and routines. It's a time for celebration, especially when students can articulate their own needs and growth.

On the next page, you'll find reflection responses from students in October, after they'd written every day since the beginning of August.

What questions might I ask to track or highlight changes from the beginning of the year?

- What daily habits are important for growing writers?
- What's the student's attitude toward writing?
- What's fun about writing?
- What's challenging?
- What types of writing are most engaging?
- What's not so much fun in relation to writing?
- What questions do students have about writing?
- What would make writing more fun?

How have you grown as a writer since August? Has your attitude toward writing changed, and if so, how?

"I have two ways I have grown. One, I like poems because I like to write in a different way. Two, I like to write fiction stories because it's fun to write things that don't actually happen in real life (but could)!" —Bella

"How my attitude has changed is that I used to hate to write and now I love to because I can write down my feelings and feel relieved." —Hudson

"I now don't have to ask for ideas, and now I think of them myself!" —Prince

"My attitude toward writing hasn't really changed since August. It always amazes me how much power a paper and pencil can have." —Anne Clare

What's your favorite thing about writing?

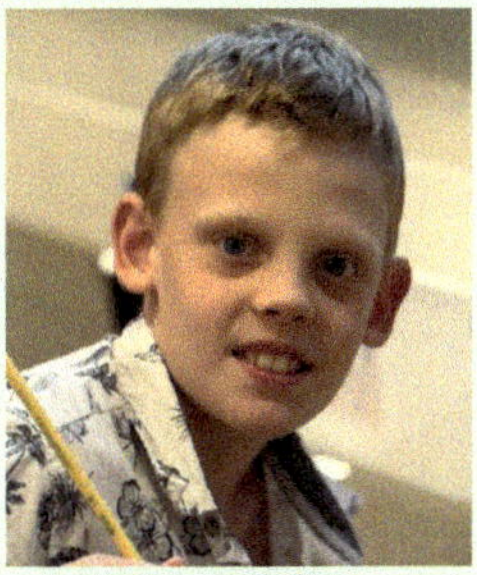

"My #1 thing about writing is writing realistic fiction graphic novels. I also love writing fantasy. Who knew?!" —Colton

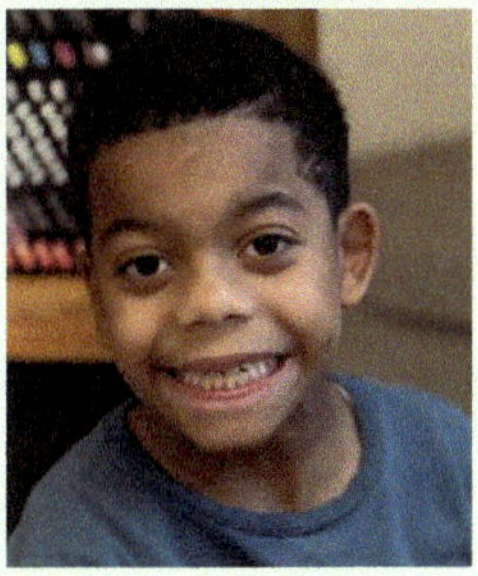

"I love writing poetry. I love how I can craft words into songs." —Lorenzo

What are your hopes for writing and reading this semester?

"I hope we keep on doing more writing and art and continue showing our writing to other people." —Malea

Even though we haven't had whole-class genre studies on every genre or type of writing mentioned by the kids, what's important to note is that there is time for experimentation and playfulness in writing each day, time to try things out in their writer's notebooks, time to read the genres they would most love to write, and time to talk about the plans they have for future writing and to share in-process work with friends and with me.

When writers know that I honor their thinking and see their ideas as opportunities for growth and celebration, they're more likely to feel trusted and be honest in their responses. With that belief in place, the writers say what's in their heart and what they truly believe and need as writers, readers, and people.

Ensuring that ALL Writers Have Access and Tools They Need to Be Successful

Being a writer doesn't only mean flourishing with a pencil and paper in hand. Honoring and highlighting the multifaceted, multimodal opportunities that writers have to get their voices in the world is another important part of asset lens assessment. Be intentional about lifting and bringing to the forefront all the ways writers share their ideas.

Some writers use sign language to get their ideas out into the world. Other writers need audio recording devices to speak and translate their work for others to listen to and enjoy. Some writers draw and paint to best communicate their ideas. Some writers need partners to support and enhance their work. Some writers collect and build with tools and materials to share their stories and ideas. It's imperative that we see *all* students as writers and celebrate them as writers, no matter what form of communication or modality they need to be successful.

Mariana works in her notebook. She sometimes wears noise canceling headphones when writing to concentrate.

Documenting Joy and Freedom in Photographs

I was reminded of the sheer power of documenting joy and freedom in our writing classrooms through photos from Angela's Stockman's book, *The Writing Teacher's Guide to Pedagogical Documentation* (2024). This practice gives me the opportunity to reflect on what's happening under the surface of that joy. What practices are in place that give rise to that joy and freedom, and how might we make space for more of those opportunities?

If You Want to Learn More about Documenting Student Growth and Asset Lens Assessment...

Troublemakers: Lessons in Freedom from Young Children at School, Carla Shalaby (2017)

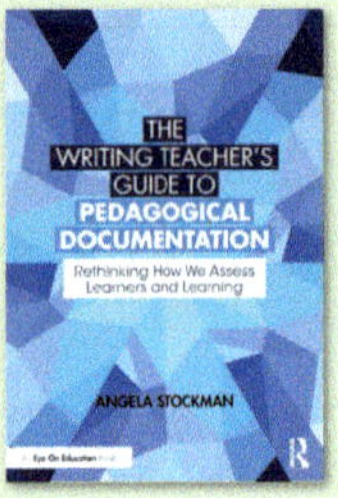

The Writing Teacher's Guide to Pedagogical Documentation: Rethinking How We Assess Learners and Learning, Angela Stockman (2024)

Conclusion

In these pages, I hope that you've found energy, joy, practical applications for your own classroom, respect for our profession, and trust in the children who guide us every day. How we see children affects how we teach them. If we see them as people and writers first and honor their voices and identities, our classrooms will become spaces where they flourish and grow.

My work and my own learning wouldn't be possible without this group of beautiful children, the 42 fourth-grade writers at Vestavia Hills Elementary, Cahaba Heights.

We thank you for coming alongside us on this journey through the first weeks of school.

May we all find daily opportunities to teach and learn alongside our students in classrooms of freedom, ones that fill the souls of writers with oxygen, nourishment, and joy.

About the Author

For the past 30 years, Ann Marie Corgill has been a classroom teacher, learning alongside elementary students in grades 1–6. A fierce advocate for children, she believes in co-creating classroom spaces where every child's heart and mind is nurtured, their voices and ideas are amplified, and their days are filled with joy, curiosity, and community.

She has served on NCTE's Elementary Section Steering Committee and as the Elementary Representative-at-Large on NCTE's Executive Committee. A former Alabama Teacher of the Year and National Teacher of the Year Finalist, Ann Marie is a National Board Certified Teacher and the author of *Of Primary Importance: What's Essential in Teaching Young Writers.*

Ann Marie is currently working as a library-media specialist, sharing a love of literature and learning with the readers, writers, and changemakers at Vestavia Hills Elementary, Dolly Ridge, in Alabama.